The IDEA Guide to the
2012 U.S. Presidential Debates

The IDEA Guide to the 2012 U.S. Presidential Debates

International Debate Education Association

New York, London & Amsterdam

Published in 2012 by
The International Debate Education Association
105 East 22nd Street Suite 915
New York, NY 10010

This book is published with the generous support of the Open
Society Foundations

ISBN 978-1-61770-060-6

Design by Kathleen Hayes
Printed in the United States of America

Contents

Performing Democracy: American Presidential Debates

Bruce Lee Zellers

Service Above Ambition (1800–1830)

Although airplanes, cell phones, and Twitter would likely evoke wonder among the Founding Fathers, perhaps nothing would shock them more than the modern presidential election campaign. They would surely disapprove of the frenetic, 24/7 efforts to win the office and the central role played by the candidates themselves. The Founders would think that modern campaigns focus too much on the personalities of the candidates, and often not enough on the great issues of the day. The thought of a public confrontation in the form of debates between candidates would have struck many of the Founders as both inappropriate and undesirable. While eighteenth-century politicians debated vigorously in assemblies, congresses, and conventions, including the Constitutional Convention, actual campaigning for offices was viewed with suspicion in the rural communities most Americans inhabited at the time. Americans saw office-*holding* as service to one's neighbors, but office-*seeking* was a sign of ambition and self-promotion. In the early Republic this distinction applied particularly to the presidency. Candidates for president did not tour the nation seeking votes; they did not give speeches or make appearances. They neither attacked their opponents nor offered agendas of their own. In many respects they remained detached from the voter, both personally and professionally. It is hard to imagine any of the Founders running for president today—and harder still to imagine them winning.

For most of the first decade under the Constitution, the Federalists and Democratic Republicans, the two political parties at the time, had been locked in a fierce debate over the economic and political future of the United States. Jefferson's party, the Democratic Republicans, insisted that the United States remain primarily a nation of farmers overseen by a weak central government; the Federalists, the party of George Washington, John Adams, and Alexander Hamilton, sought a nation where commerce and industry were the dominant economic activities and a strong central government oversaw their health. In his famous book *Democracy in America*, Alexis de Tocqueville, the French political thinker, would define this as a debate between "great" parties, an argument over the "principles upon which the government is to be conducted." Yet Jefferson stayed at home during the key confrontation, the election of 1800. In his mind, the office must seek the man—active pursuit of the presidency would be unacceptable. As biographer Dumas Malone tells us, in Jefferson's Virginia, "participation in matters of local government was as much a part of the normal business of life as practicing law or cultivating his farms; or, as Jefferson once argued to friends, 'the desires of others had obliged him to go into an office he nei-ther liked nor wanted.'"

Fortunately, offices did seek him, for, as Malone points out, "Jefferson was not good at electioneering or at mingling with a crowd." Thus, in 1800, "Jefferson himself played virtually no direct part in the campaign," according to Malone. A later writer, Merrill Peterson, adds that "he was a passive and, on the whole, silent observer of the presidential campaign." He was not present at the caucus that nominated him, gave no speeches, and wrote nothing for publication during the cam-paign. He even delayed responding to letters. Malone asserts that this strategy allowed Jefferson to maintain his dignity and keep his hands clean. He delegated the day-to-day work of winning an election to "friends" and party managers such as John Beckley. The real business of the election was gaining electoral votes—and the electors were chosen by the state legislatures. Thus, winning legislative majorities was the key task. Politics were local and local committees distributed infor-mation and sought to influence the voters who would choose state legislators. According to Peterson, the first election song came from these efforts: "Jefferson and Liberty."

Voting by the states was staggered, mostly in October and November. Jefferson had to wait for the outcome, spending his days checking the votes. As in all presidential elections, hyper-bole and personal attacks played a role; frightening voters was already a well-established tactic. Jefferson was accused of being un-American and of being an enemy of Christianity. The charge that he had had a sexual relationship with one of his slaves, Sally Hemings, appeared in the next election cycle. Every election sometimes seems worse than the last in this respect, but Malone asserts, "the personal attacks on Jeffer-son were the most vicious in any presidential campaign on record." As we said, he was a sensitive man, so these smears hurt, but he nursed his wounds in private. To Malone, Jefferson's behavior in this critical election illustrates that he had "not wholly thrown off the distrust of parties he had inherited from the past and had not ceased to dislike squabbling" and divisive partisanship.

Many of the Founders believed that political parties—often called "factions" in the terminology of the day—imperiled the nation. As James Madison wrote in the famous tenth essay of *The Federalist*, factions were a natural response to differing interests and might, and therefore they have a role to play in the political system, especially at the state level. At the national level, however, they must be discouraged; too much power was at stake. Madison hoped that the size of the nation and the design of the Constitution might counteract the spirit of faction or party. But Madison was not alone in believing that presidents, who he said must be "above party," must work against that spirit as well. According to historian Ralph Ketcham, the Founders were under the influence of Henry Bolingbroke's, "On the Idea of a Patriot King." Bolingbroke, an Englishman writing more than a generation earlier, argued that kings should be unifiers; they should work to benefit the nation as a whole. Good kings separated themselves from all narrow interests and all political groups. Bolingbroke was suspicious of individualism, the pursuit of personal opportunity, and the idea of majority rule. When published in England in 1749, it already reflected an eccentric, somewhat outdated vision for England. And Bolingbroke's imagined nation of unified communities possessing a "common good" certainly did not describe the dynamic, diverse society developing in the United States in the age of the Founders. Their attraction to Bolingbroke and other Enlightenment-era writers suggests that the Founders were at something of a transitional point in Western intellectual history, a place between the medieval past and the more modern, democratic future.

Jefferson was drawn to Bolingbroke, and the Englishman's social and political views put the American in an awkward spot. Jefferson, as well as many others of his generation, believed that leaders were to display "virtue," or, as they liked to say, "civic virtue." Leaders must be detached from all "lower motives": personal ambition, the desire for economic gain, or even a concern for personal comfort. Jefferson himself wrote in a letter to John Garland Jefferson, "In a government like ours, it is the duty of the Chief Magistrate, in order to enable himself to do all the good which his station requires . . . to unite in himself the confidence of the whole people." The president's job, according to Jefferson, was to set a "moral example" and to "articulate national goals" so as to improve the lives of all citizens. It must be much more than an executive position. Presidents must "espouse no party, but govern like the common father of his people." Jefferson, in his first inaugural address, put it this way: "We are all Federalists, we are all Republicans." These notions, a manifestation of republican hopes and ideals, left candidate and party leader Jefferson in a position where it was difficult to participate in partisan campaigning.

Of course, Jefferson was not alone in these difficulties. Alexander Hamilton, writing in support of the ratification of the Constitution in *The Federalist* under the Roman name Publius, shared similar views. He described the process of choosing a Chief Magistrate as an "appointment," rather than an "election." He hoped that the process might be carried on in "circumstances favorable to deliberation" and that it might avoid "tumult and disorder" as well as "heats and ferments."

Based on these comments, Publius would certainly not have approved of our presidential campaigns!

The awkward fit between these concepts and other aspects of American political ideology is striking. How does, for example, the Jeffersonian belief in an executive free of party affiliation affect notions of individual rights and the desire to grant individual consent? What about the belief in majority rule, praised by Jefferson in his first inaugural? The first six presidents, according to Ketcham, struggled to be simultaneously above parties and within them. Jefferson, in his view, displayed extraordinary skill and perseverance in gathering and guiding willing followers, without "leading" them in a conventional way. The erosion of this vision of presidents being above politics and its replacement by a model of presidents enmeshed in politics, brought about by both ideological and technological change, is the theme of this article.

Initially, the nation's communications infrastructure reinforced the desire for decentralized, locally oriented campaigns. Americans were isolated from one another. The basic transportation system inherited from the colonies remained in place. News traveled little faster than it had in 1756 or 1776, and people did, too: both the Constitutional Convention and the new federal government it created opened a month late because of travel difficulties. It took George Washington eight days to get from Mount Vernon to New York City in order to take up the presidency. Two years later, the trip from Monticello to New York both bored and exhausted Thomas Jefferson. According to Merrill Peterson, he "buffeted along at a pace of five or six miles an hour" for 20 days. Or consider the time it took to deliver the mail: in 1789 a letter from Portland, Maine, to Savannah, Georgia, took 40 days; a letter from Philadelphia to Lexington, Kentucky, took 32 days. And while the nation possessed perhaps two hundred newspapers in 1800, their readership was local; no national media yet existed. Thus, the ability of any politician to coordinate strategy or even campaign themes was severely limited. All of this helps to explain why, in 1800, the Democratic Republicans failed to coordinate the casting of electoral votes. Jefferson and Aaron Burr ended up in a tie that required 37 ballots in Congress to resolve.

But change came rapidly in the nineteenth century. An efficient national community came into existence, one where people and information moved much more rapidly. The Post Office played an enormous role in this process. In 1792 Congress passed the Post Office Act, which facilitated the flow of information around the country. The Act led to the rapid increase in the number of post offices around the nation: 75 in 1790, 903 in 1800, and 13,468 in 1840. Those who created this new service desired speedy deliveries, and the Post Office responded: by 1839 the delivery time of a letter from Portland to Savannah had dropped to 12 days and a letter from Philadelphia to Lexington took just 8 days. The Post Office subsidized the delivery of newspapers in order to foster democracy, creating a national market for information. The number of papers and magazines increased dramatically—newspapers remained locally oriented institutions—as Americans became avid newspaper readers. Politicians knew a good thing when they saw it: congressional speeches were mailed free of charge (a system called "franking"). These changes enlarged and enlivened the public sphere. The spread of the telegraph, first used in 1844, further enhanced the flow of information around the nation; within two years much of the east coast of the United States was connected, and by 1861 telegraph lines had reached California. Telephones followed at the end of the century. The age of instant communications had dawned.

People moved more rapidly, especially by rail. In 1850, only 9,000 miles of track existed, but by 1860 more than 30,000 miles of track connected America's cities. By 1900 there were nearly 200,000 miles. But travel was still not comfortable. In February, 1860, Abraham Lincoln traveled from his home in Springfield, Illinois, to New York City to give a speech that he hoped would enhance his candidacy for the presidency. He rode on five different trains, changing three times after midnight. One train arrived four hours late. No food was available on these trains, which were also cold and drafty. He arrived in New York just as Jefferson had seventy years earlier: exhausted. By the twentieth century, the Pennsylvania Railroad's Broadway Limited passenger train made the Chicago–New York trip in just twenty hours, with no train changes required. Within a few more years, the travel time was reduced to 16 hours, a mere jaunt compared to 1860. These technological improvements in transportation and communication created the prerequisites for mass political parties. And, of course, they also offered new opportunities for presidential candidates.

From Stump Speeches to Whistle-Stop Tours (1830–1912)

The great democratic revolution that swept over the United States in the first third of the nineteenth century significantly eroded the Founders' desire for a president above politics and parties. Ironically, Jeffersonian beliefs drove this development. After the Revolution the ideals of equality and liberty percolated through American society. Historian Bernard Bailyn calls the phenomenon the "contagion of liberty." Nowhere was this revolution more visible than in the extension of the right to vote to virtually all white males over the age of 21. States set voting requirements, so this change occurred gradually, state by state. Mobilizing and organizing this mass of voters, especially for presidential elections, became the central task of political parties. In the 1830s, Andrew Jackson and his supporters began to not just defend parties, but to advocate for them as a necessary mechanism for empowering democracy. In a fateful step, new state laws shifted the power to choose presidential electors from the legislatures to the voters. These changes posed a significant challenge to the political philosophy of the Founders. Democracy began to politicize the presidency.

Presidential elections became a combination of carnival, festival, and circus. Campaigns featured speeches, slogans, parades, posters, banners, barbecues, flags, and special newspapers—whatever would energize voters and get them to the polls. Catch slogans—the precursor to our sound bites—supplemented or even replaced more reasoned considerations of the issues. Thus, in 1840 the Whigs gave the American political lexicon "Tippecanoe and Tyler too," a reference to Whig candidates William Henry Harrison, the victor at the Battle of Tippecanoe, and his running mate John Tyler. The Whigs also showed us how misrepresentation, not just by the opposition but also by political parties wanting to paint their own candidate a certain way, could become central to presidential campaigns: they dubbed William Henry Harrison the "log cabin and hard cider candidate" in an effort to depict him as a man of the people, even though Harrison had come from a wealthy, prominent Virginia family.

Campaigns developed dramatic narratives and scenes that resembled theater, and they rewarded politicians who also had a flair for performance. Volunteers and paid campaign

f the work. As the century advanced, the
⌣ behind-the-scenes operatives sometimes took
⌣er hue. Historian Mark Summers explains that late-
⌣eenth-century campaigns featured fake quotes, gossip, and efforts to generate the "politics of outrage" by connecting opponents to foreign governments. It was "war without bayonets." Both major parties bought votes and transported voters to districts where they were needed. Summers writes: "Vote buying was not one of the dirty secrets of Gilded Age politics. It was done out in the open." This was not the thoughtful procedure Publius had hoped for. In Richard McCormick's view, it "bore little resemblance to that which had been contemplated by the Framers" and revealed the "continuing tension between the republican ideal" and democratic realities. American presidential campaigns were not for the genteel, the thoughtful, or the squeamish; Edwin L. Godwin lamented in 1896 that "the Campaign is simply disgusting. We shall win, but what a victory!" Presidential campaigns were football, rather than golf. Tocqueville, observing the American electoral process in its opening stages, had predicted that great parties and significant elections would henceforth be rare in America. Instead, he predicted that our electoral battles would seem childish to outsiders; they would abound with "lesser controversy" and the "ambitions of leaders." The big questions became: How would presidents and presidential candidates shape their behaviors in this environment? Would they embrace the energy and open competitiveness of American democracy, or would they resist them?

The election of 1860 illustrates the complex relationships candidates developed with these emerging political practices. Rarely has there been a more consequential political clash. North and South were on the verge of separation. The

Democratic Party, the party of Jackson, had split into northern and southern wings because of slavery. Southern Democrats threatened to leave the nation if the voters chose the Republican candidate, Abraham Lincoln. A third-party candidate, John Bell, also appeared. Amid this crisis, Abraham Lincoln's strategy owed more to Jefferson than to Jackson. He was a forceful, articulate candidate, delivering both effective stump speeches (impromptu talks given to local audiences and delivered with folksy charm) and memorable formal addresses, such as the one he gave at the Cooper Union earlier in 1860. And, of course, he was a skilled debater, as the Lincoln-Douglas debates of 1858 proved. Lincoln and incumbent senator Stephen Douglas were competing for a Senate seat in Illinois; the victor would be decided by the Illinois legislature after statewide elections in November. (Direct election of senators came with the Seventeenth Amendment in 1913.) Lincoln, the rising star, challenged his better-known Democratic opponent to a series of debates around the state, and Douglas accepted. They met seven times between August and October, each debate taking place in a different city and both men traveling by road and rail. Each clash drew 10,000–20,000 people and was prefaced by the hoopla that voters now expected: parades, banners, bands, and cannon fire. Both Lincoln and Douglas practiced the arts of personal attack and misrepresentation. Each candidate spoke for ninety minutes and delivered elaborate, extended arguments. The debates were all recorded by reporters (who often produced transcripts tailored for their partisan audiences) and distributed around the nation by telegraph. Lincoln lost in 1858, but he returned in 1860 for the next round with Douglas, running for president in that year's election.

When Lincoln and Douglas competed again in the 1860 presidential campaign, the main issue was once more the future of slavery in the United States. This time, Lincoln went with a strategy similar to that of his great hero Jefferson two generations earlier: he chose a non-campaign. He did not attend the Republican convention in Chicago, did not over-see the content of the party's platform, and made no effort to influence the choice of the vice presidential candidate. He relied on the energy and discretion of his campaign manager, David Davis. He learned of his nomination by telegraph in his hometown of Springfield, Illinois and also stayed home for the campaign. As historian Stephen Oates explains: "He did no campaigning himself, relying on Republican workers to dis-seminate his printed speeches."

Those workers certainly did their jobs: the nation was blanketed with images of "The Rail Splitter," entertained by parades, educated by an array of paid speakers, and fed at barbecues. As in most American elections, bitter invective was a part of the campaign: opponents called Lincoln "vulgar," "illiterate," "blood thirsty," "horrid looking," "scoundrelly," and, of course, "unqualified." Lincoln's patriotism was attacked because he had opposed the war with Mexico in the 1840s. And he was accused of desiring racial integration. Lincoln gave no speeches and there was no second round of Lincoln-Doug-las debates. The candidate stayed close to home, observing events through newspapers and telegraph, writing letters, seeing a steady stream of visitors that included reporters and photographers, and keeping track of the balloting from the Springfield telegraph office. The Founders would have approved of this approach. It was Douglas who stretched tra-dition: he traveled around the nation by train, hoping to rally Democrats against Lincoln and, after losing the election, he traveled additional miles in an effort to keep the South from seceding and the nation from falling into civil war.

The heated election of 1896 shows us that Lincoln's strategy of 1860 would be employed again with similarly successful results and that upholding the Founders' tradition of remaining above politics could still pay electoral dividends. However, the campaign also suggests the way campaigns were being transformed. Social and economic changes were the underlying issues; modernization was reshaping the country. The new urban and industrial America, symbolized by titans of industry like Andrew Carnegie and John D. Rockefeller, was superseding the rural/agricultural America symbolized by Jefferson and Madison. Increasingly, business leaders looked to the Republicans to represent their needs. What business wanted and Republicans offered was selective laissez-faire economics: very limited federal oversight of railroads, working conditions, and product quality, but high tariffs on imported goods that competed with products produced by Carnegie, Rockefeller, and company. The Republicans also promised a gold currency, which would help business investors at the expense of farmers.

For their part, the farmers formed a range of organizations, such as the Grange, the Farmers Alliances, and the People's Party, to pursue their needs. The farmers wanted radical changes and they were willing to use the federal government to protect their interests and advance their program. Injured by the railroads' land use policies, they spoke of nationalizing them. They lobbied for the unlimited coinage of silver as their panacea, believing that it would cause currency inflation, which would improve farm incomes. Western farmers had given up on the Democrats and the Republicans; in 1892 they founded the People's Party (often called the Populists).

This organization attracted a host of colorful characters, many of whom were fervent evangelical Protestants. Their program flirted with socialism and served as a prelude to the later progressive movement. In 1892 their presidential candidate, James B. Weaver, won a million votes (8.5 percent of the total) and earned 22 electoral votes, while the party elected a number of state and local officials. They looked forward to 1896, when big issues would be on the table. This had the makings of a great contest.

However, the candidates debated those great issues only indirectly and sporadically. The Republicans nominated Ohio governor William McKinley, who was a militant advocate of the Grand Old Party's ideas. Campaigning did not intimidate him in the slightest: in 1894 McKinley undertook a nationwide speaking tour to defend the tariff policies of his party; as his biographer Kevin Phillips tells us, McKinley delivered almost four hundred speeches in three hundred cities. But in 1896 he stayed above the fray, wanting to reflect the ideal of the Founders that "the office should seek the man." He followed the example of Grover Cleveland, a Democrat, who learned of his nomination in 1884 by telephone as he worked at his desk as New York's governor, only accepting the nomination formally in an address two months later. Cleveland then played only a minor role in his own election, delivering just four speeches. The strategy worked: Cleveland won.

McKinley used the same playbook. He, too, learned of his nomination by telephone. His campaign was calm and low-key. Rather than giving speeches, he stayed home in Canton, Ohio, and allowed the Republican Party to bring voters to him. He greeted each visiting group from his front porch. Each got a smile and brief remarks; serious issues were avoided. In fact, the Republicans produced a short film (a campaign first) showing the relaxed candidate chatting with citizens in front of that famous porch. The real work of the campaign was done by hundreds of paid agents who distributed 120 million pieces of campaign literature (in nine languages), the most extensive public information effort by a presidential campaign yet. In cities, workers joined in huge pro-Republican rallies—after getting the day off from their bosses.

His opponent, William Jennings Bryan, on the other hand, waged an aggressive, public, and very personal campaign. Bryan was a rising Democratic politician whose speeches, incorporating both Jeffersonian ideology and the theology of evangelical Protestantism, had won him fervent support on the Great Plains. Bryan played a key role in becoming his party's candidate. He attended the Democratic convention in Chicago, helped shape the party platform, and then clinched his own nomination with a moving speech in which he delivered his famous line decrying the gold standard: "You shall not crucify mankind on a cross of gold!" The Populists, who had run their own candidate in 1892, joined with the Democrats in nominating Bryan. Bryan then vigorously and unapologetically sought the office. According to biographer Michael Kazin, Bryan traveled 18,000 miles by rail, gave 250 speeches (and many more minor greetings in small towns where his train stopped), visited 26 states, and addressed 5 million people.

But while Bryan was himself central to his campaign, he still had to rely on paid agents and speakers. Speeches were published and distributed. McKinley's positions were misrepresented, and votes were bought. Unfortunately for Bryan and his supporters, they had only one-tenth of the money available to their opponent. In this campaign, Bryan showed clearly that presidential candidates who openly sought the presidency needed the skills of performers. Each speech was memorable, a theatrical *tour de force*. He wrote his own mate-rial and rehearsed it thoroughly. Kazin tells us that Bryan's delivery was vigorous, sincere, sentimental and, perhaps most important of all, positive. Audiences believed that he spoke from the heart. Yet he aimed not just to entertain or to move, but to convince. He wanted to change the nation. The issues were huge and America's responses to them would determine "the fate of the nation and the welfare of 'humanity.'" He had spent much of his life debating, and now he sought to put those skills to work in a debate with McKinley, but conven-tion dictated that it be indirect. McKinley made no effort to debate, or even to reply systematically from his front porch to whatever charges were lobbed at him. Despite Bryan's stren-uous efforts, McKinley could be provoked into little beyond platitudes. In the end, the campaign teams from both par-ties flooded voters with materials offering sharply polarized visions. The election of 1896, like so many others, was not really a debate, but more an example of parallel advertising campaigns.

The 1912 campaign probably came closer to presenting an explicit candidate debate than any campaign before 1960. The central issue in this contest was how best to deal with the problems of industrialization, which included the concen-trated economic power of a small elite, the poverty of millions of Americans, and the waste of natural resources. The incum-bent president, Republican William Howard Taft, had attracted the hostility of his predecessor and one-time supporter, Theo-dore Roosevelt, with his caution and conservatism. Roosevelt sought far more energetic federal responses to the nation's problems. Denied the Republican nomination despite a string of primary victories, Roosevelt and his supporters founded the Progressive Party and he ran as its nominee for President. The

Democratic Party nominated New Jersey Governor and former Princeton president Woodrow Wilson. The well-known socialist Eugene V. Debs constituted the final major candidate. In the words of historian John Milton Cooper, the resulting contest was "one of the great campaigns in American history."

It quickly became a two-candidate race. Debs was largely ignored by the political establishment; Taft gave just two speeches and let the party activists carry the burden of a losing campaign. The more procedurally conservative Wilson upheld a longstanding tradition by not attending his party's convention and by only acknowledging his nomination in a speech a month later. Roosevelt, on the other hand, delivered a powerful speech to the Progressive Party convention in Chicago and played a key role in shaping the party platform.

The views of the two men differed strikingly. Roosevelt asserted that the nation's problems could only be resolved through the enlargement of federal power, especially the power to regulate business activity. As he said in his convention speech, there is "but one institution which we can use effectively against the colossal power of business and that institution is the government of the United States." He would call his ideology the New Nationalism. Wilson, on the other hand, railed against what he considered Rooseveltian paternalism and elitism, arguing that the chief task of government is to challenge institutions that imperil freedom, not to regulate business. He would call his ideology the New Freedom. Roosevelt and Wilson were the "heirs of Hamilton and Jefferson," according to historian James Chance. John Cooper agrees: "For the only time except perhaps for Jefferson's first election in 1800, a presidential campaign aired questions that verged on political philosophy. It was a remarkable moment." Both men were committed to "passionately intense, wide-ranging, and philosophically rich debates about the purposes and directions of American . . . politics." They brought seriousness, depth, and sophistication to the task. Both men saw the "education of the public as the most important ingredient of political leadership." Roosevelt often focused on facts and specifics, while Wilson, the college professor, preferred philosophy. Roosevelt, in particular, relished rapid and direct responses to Wilson's speeches; his staff "arranged to keep him informed of what Wilson was saying" so that the candidate could keep his remarks fresh and timely. Compared to the typical American presidential campaign, seriousness pervaded this one: while neither man wholly avoided opportunistic misrepresentations, neither indulged in intemperate remarks concerning his opponent either.

However, this was an indirect debate, as had been the case in all previous campaigns. The traditions and practices of the political community, coupled with the realities of early twentieth- century campaigning, kept the candidates from appearing on the same platform. Even if they had appeared on the same stage, such an event would not have reached enough voters to sway a national election. In fact, the two men met only once during the campaign season, in Princeton, New Jersey, in May 1912, when Wilson observed an outdoor Roosevelt rally from the back of the crowd. Cooper writes, "that was the closest Roosevelt and Wilson came to a face-to-face debate at any time in their careers." Instead, both men made use of the nation's impressive rail network to travel the country independently. In the age before radio and television, travel was the only way to bring the candidates directly to the voters. The pattern looked something like this: a series of major speeches was scheduled, at a state fair, for instance. Celebrities such as Thomas Edison sometimes appeared with the candidate. As the candidate's train moved from city to city, it stopped briefly in small towns along the way where the candidate offered some locally inflected conventional remarks, welcomed local officials on the train for a few miles, and then departed. Bryan had perfected the technique, called whistle-stopping because candidates often made speeches from the train when it stopped at the station.

The candidates experienced great physical stress. At one point, Roosevelt delivered 20 speeches in a single day. Both candidates spoke in front of large crowds without amplification: Roosevelt addressed 20,000 people in Boston and 50,000 in St. Paul; Wilson spoke to 25,000 people in Indianapolis and perhaps 100,000 in Chicago. Roosevelt ultimately visited 34 states and traveled 10,000 miles by train and automobile. Both men lost their voices—and Roosevelt traveled with a voice specialist. Even plagued by hoarseness, these men, like Bryan before them, held the voters' attention by employing the tools of drama. They were great performers. Wilson could put people in a trance, but no one could equal Roosevelt's energy and timing. In mid-October Roosevelt was scheduled to give a speech in Milwaukee. On his way there by car, he was shot and wounded. The wound would have been more serious if the folded speech in his pocket had not slowed the bullet. On the stage, he displayed his bloody shirt and proclaimed, "it is hard to kill a bull moose," invoking the nickname of the Progressive Party. His subsequent absence from campaigning while he recovered to full health may have cost him the election.

The campaign ended in a near-debate. Both candidates spoke at Madison Square Garden in New York, but on alternate nights: Roosevelt to 15,000 people on October 30, Wilson to a similarly sized crowd on October 31. Wilson won the election;

the turnout was just 59 percent of the eligible voters (for Bryan/McKinley it was 79 percent). Had all of the words, all of the travel, and all of the hoopla made any difference in the end? John Cooper thinks not: "One of the most exciting campaigns in American history, fought between the two most attractive available candidates and over hotly debated issues, failed to change many votes. The winner in 1912 was politics as usual."

Technology Unites the Electorate (1913–1959)

Beginning in second third of the twentieth century, communications technology made possible access to millions of potential voters simultaneously and in real time; radio, and later television, thereby transformed presidential campaigns at least as dramatically as the post office and the railroads had in the nineteenth century. The possibility of face-to-face debates between presidential candidates became greater. Franklin Roosevelt's campaigns in the 1930s and 1940s marked a transition from addressing the voters directly in modest crowds to addressing them in huge numbers virtually. However, it was still too early for same-stage debates between candidates. The election of 1932 occurred amidst the worst economic and social circumstances in the nation's history. The stock market crash of October 1929 had ushered in a collapse of the banking system and the stoppage of much of the industrial economy. In 1932 the nation's overall unemployment rate reached 25 percent, but much greater suffering occurred in particular places. In Ohio, for example, the unemployment rate was 37 percent in 1932 according to the Ohio Historical Society, while in the manufacturing city of Toledo, 80 percent of the industrial workforce searched for work. Thousands of veterans came to Washington, DC, seeking advances on bonuses promised to them for their service in World War I, but they were dispersed by soldiers. In rural areas, farmers destroyed crops and armed themselves to prevent foreclosures. In a number of cities, the hungry demanded food and work. President Herbert Hoover, a well-known humanitarian in his pre-presidential days and a sophisticated advocate of laissez-faire Republican policies in the 1920s (the "New Era"), was now blamed for the Depression and was mocked by having his name attached to many forms of suffering: Hoovervilles (shantytowns constructed out of boxes, crates, and scraps of metal), Hoover blankets (newspapers), and Hoover flags (empty pockets hanging out of pants). You might have thought it was time for another spirited campaign debate like that of 1912. As it happened, neither candidate wanted it.

The Republicans re-nominated Hoover without enthusiasm. Today, he and his party often appear in our memories as unimaginative conservatives. However, in many respects, they had eagerly embraced modern developments. Hoover himself was not just wealthy, but media savvy; he knew how public relations worked and he had used them to shape his public image. Party leaders were also open to new techniques. In 1920, for instance, they had employed Albert Lasker, an advertising professional, to "sell" Warren G. Harding, that year's Republican candidate for president. They experimented with radio, film, audio records, and photo-ops with the candidate, even as they employed tried and true tactics: coverage in newspapers and magazines and on billboards. However, in his 1928 campaign for the presidency, Hoover had chosen the conservative strategy, an approach William McKinley would have recognized. It was the familiar pattern of the candidate being above politics. Hoover did not formally acknowledge his nomination for two months. His campaign consisted of just seven speeches that focused mostly on praising the Republican platform. He said little about his Democratic opponent, Al Smith. The nation was prosperous; there were no major issues.

In 1932 the situation was different, of course. The Depression was now three years old and the public was angry. Hoover's record was under attack. However, the candidate and his party chose to use a modified traditional strategy. Again, Hoover acknowledged his nomination two months after it had occurred. This time, though, he traveled around a bit more. He spoke over the radio, despite the fact that he was audibly uncomfortable with the medium. He delivered a series of speeches, some of which bitterly refuted the attacks by Roosevelt, most of which, however, were dull, filled with statistics, and burdened with platitudes, according to his biographer, David Burner. Hoover's speeches employed words unfamiliar to the vast majority of listeners, like "Sisyphean," "vacuous," "supervened," and "palpably," and they rarely offered new ideas. In fact, he indulged in hyperbole and what Burner calls "contemptible appeal[s] to fear." Hoover accused his opponent of being a radical socialist, or worse. According to one skeptical Republican cited by Burner, "Hoover stimulated fears of what FDR might do because it was his only way to overcome feelings of hatred for himself." Many audiences headed for the exits early. In Detroit, residents didn't want him to start: a mob met him at the train station. Burner observes, "politics . . . [is] a game of power; to the naive Hoover, it was a solemn obligation for public service." The Founders would have understood.

According to historian James MacGregor Burns, the two candidates in 1932 presented very different images to the public: Franklin Roosevelt was "a man in motion," while Hoover was "a man stuck fast." Like many previous candidates, Roosevelt did not attend the Democratic National Convention in Chicago; he followed the ebb and flow of his chances for the nomination by way of the radio. Once the party had nominated him, however, he became more innovative. He chartered a Ford Trimotor aircraft (think Indiana Jones in China in 1935) and flew to Chicago to accept the nomination. It was a dreadful flight, cold and slow, and it arrived hours late in Chicago. However, after a festive motorcade to the convention site, he asserted to the delegates that he wanted to avoid "hypocrisy and sham." Burns quotes the future president: "Let it also be symbolic that in doing so [flying to Chicago] I broke traditions. Let it be said that from now on the task of our party is to break foolish traditions and leave it to the Republican leaders, far more skilled in the art, to break promises."

Some elements of the campaign reflected this stirring call. Roosevelt was very comfortable in front of microphones and gave many effective radio broadcasts. But much of the campaign was less innovative. It began, of course, with mobilizing thousands of campaign workers to mail pamphlets, hang posters, and otherwise energize the voters. And the candidate spent much of the fall on trains, just as Bryan and Theodore Roosevelt had done. He owned the whistle stop strategy, and loved meeting and bantering with voters and local officials. He delivered sixty major speeches, each one typically devoted to a separate topic: in Topeka it was agriculture, for instance. He attacked Hoover, but offered little to suggest what his so-called New Deal might consist of because he did not know at that point. The two candidates never met and the nature of the campaign itself emphasized little beyond personality. It may have looked like 1912, but conceptually it was quite different. On election eve tradition was again upheld: like Lincoln, Roosevelt learned of his election victory in his own home, in Hyde Park, New York.

Four years later, in his race against Kansas governor Alfred M. Landon, Roosevelt again embraced tradition, even as he stretched it. In 1936 he vigorously defended the New Deal and suggested the direction of future reform. He saw himself as locked in battle with the forces of conservatism — and he was determined to defeat them. Roosevelt dominated every aspect of the convention, from the wording of the platform defending his first term, to the order and content of the speeches. He listened to everything on the radio in the White House. His acceptance speech, given before 100,000 people at the Franklin Field Stadium in Philadelphia and a large radio audience, was a strong attack on economic inequality driven by the policies of the "royalists of the economic order" and a memorable defense of the New Deal. He closed with an often-quoted passage: "There is a mysterious cycle in human events. To some generations much is given. To other generations much is expected. This generation has a rendezvous with destiny!" However, he then shifted into non-partisan mode. He did a bit of "presidential" travel, observing the Dust Bowl, for instance. As he waited for the campaign to begin, he received some advice from one of his supporters, Herbert B. Swope, about the tone he should take: "To be firm without being ferocious, to be kindly rather than cold; hopeful rather than pessimistic; to be human rather than to be economic; to be insistent upon every man having a chance, and above all, to make yourself to be the President of *all* the people." Jefferson couldn't have put it better; all candidates could profit from this advice.

In late September FDR launched his offensive, traveling again by train and automobile, stirring passion in the voters. He never shared a stage or a microphone with an opponent, but he directly and forcefully answered his critics on the left and right. He was, in Burns's phrase, "an old performer" in peak form. According to historian James Burns, observers noted "the incredible swiftness with which he struck a series of almost theatrical poses." In small towns those observers noted that he was a joyous "campaigner, easy in his way with crowds, quick on the trigger, homey, laughing, waving, obviously enjoying himself." It was a great show, and his confidence was infectious. Roosevelt won in 1936 with a record-breaking margin—and without ever sharing a stage with his opponent.

In 1948 President Harry Truman took these Rooseveltian methods and made them iconic. At the beginning of the campaign Truman was widely unpopular; just under 40 percent of the public approved of his presidency. The Democratic Party had split into three factions: one led by Truman, a States' Rights faction led by Strom Thurmond, and Henry Wallace's liberal faction. The early polls indicated that the Republican candidate, former New York governor Thomas Dewey, would win easily. In a harbinger of the future, small portions of both conventions had been broadcast through the emerging medium of television. The two major candidates met only once during the campaign season: both attended the dedication of Idlewild International Airport (now JFK) in July. Dewey was so confident of victory that he limited his appearances around the country. Truman, on the other hand, campaigned forcefully, beginning with an electrifying acceptance address at the Democratic National Convention at 2 AM. He was so far down in the polls that potential donors closed their wallets; as biographer Robert Donovan tells us, the Truman effort was "continually down to its last dollar." Emergency fundraising was needed to move Truman's train out of Oklahoma City in September; many radio stations insisted on cash rather than checks before broadcasts.

But Truman made great use of these limited resources. His campaign train roamed the nation, allowing the president to connect with the public and to convey his passionate partisanship to crowds large and small. At the beginning of the campaign, in Cadillac Square in Detroit, he addressed 100,000 people. Donovan describes the candidate's language as "apocalyptic," "lurid," and "hyperbolic." "He got away with murder," almost "any charge that came into his head . . . he flung without compunction at the Republicans." He called them "gluttons of privilege" and "reactionaries," and voters loved it. Wherever he went supporters shouted, "Give 'em hell Harry." Near the end of the campaign, in St. Louis, he discarded a carefully prepared speech and, speaking from his own notes, "delivered an extemporaneous broadcast speech in a style that had [the audience] rocking." Truman won a substantial victory in November, but, to a considerable degree, neither travel nor media was responsible. Of course, Dewey's complacency played a role in his own defeat, but the bigger story was the continued importance of Democratic loyalists and union supporters who got out the vote. As Truman himself said, "labor did it."

The efforts of General Dwight Eisenhower in 1952 and 1956 continued the evolution of campaigning and of the candidates' role in seeking election. Deep anxiety about the Cold War and deep dismay about the Truman administration formed the backdrop to the election in 1952. McCarthyism, the war in Korea, and the corruption in Washington had Americans longing for change. Truman's approval ratings stood at nearly

30 percent. Eisenhower, the supreme commander in Europe during World War II, entered the contest for the Republican nomination late and faced opposition from the conservative favorite Robert A. Taft. Eisenhower was not coy about his ambitions: he came to Chicago, lobbied delegates, and, after winning the nomination, crossed the street to Taft's hotel to mend fences, an unprecedented step. However, like millions of other Americans, he watched the convention on television, which had significantly expanded its coverage since 1948. He seemed surprised that delegates to the convention did not choose the vice presidential candidate, but readily agreed to Richard Nixon as his running mate on the recommendation of party leaders. The Democratic Party also met in Chicago in 1952. Their nominee would be Adlai Stevenson, the popular Illinois governor, whose welcoming address had warmed the somewhat discouraged delegates; most expected their nominee, whoever he was, to lose against the very popular and widely trusted former general. Stevenson had little to do with his own nomination, but his acceptance speech again thrilled the convention. Stevenson hoped that the campaign would "debate issues sensibly and soberly." It was a misplaced hope.

Eisenhower ("Ike") controlled every aspect of his campaign. He was eager to launch a conventional whistle stop campaign because, at the age of 62, he felt it important to prove that he had the stamina for such an undertaking—and for the presidency. He also wanted direct contact with the American people. Ike traveled all over the country by rail, testimony to the network of track still in existence then. On the last day of the campaign, Ike traveled by train from Boston to New York City, where he would await the vote count. In all, he traveled more than 50,000 miles that fall, almost 21,000 of which were by rail, twice as many rail miles as Theodore Roosevelt traveled in 1912. Richard Nixon traveled separately, on his own train.

Ike upheld traditional campaign practices. Big "destination" speeches, often broadcast on radio and/or television, were supplemented by remarks in many small towns. In such settings he emerged, according to historian Jim Newton, as "bluff and warm," "a natural politician," and a "man of the people." Biographer Stephen Ambrose argues, "Eisenhower was the last, and one of the best, whistle stop barnstormers." Like many traditional candidates, he preferred being above politics.

Stevenson did not get the debates that he had hoped for, though the candidates did spar at a distance. Perhaps the most direct exchange involved the war in Korea. Interestingly, it was an exchange between Truman and Eisenhower, rather than Stevenson and Eisenhower. The Korean War had become, in Eisenhower biographer Jean Edward Smith's words, "a partisan issue." The stalemated war exacted substantial costs in lives and money and many Americans wanted the troops home. At a speech in Connecticut, Truman "challenged Eisenhower to offer a plan for settling the war." A week later, on October 24, Eisenhower came to the Masonic Temple in Detroit and, in front of 5,000 people and a nationwide television audience, he promised to go to Korea and to assess the situation himself. For all the technology, the exchange was strikingly like the Roosevelt-Wilson speeches of 1912. While Eisenhower himself employed a charm offensive, others carried out far less civil attacks. According to Stephen Ambrose, this election should be recalled "as one of the bitterest campaigns of the 20th century." Ike was accused of being a Catholic, a Jew, and a Communist; Stevenson was accused of homosexuality. Like many of his predecessors, this side of the campaign occasionally embarrassed Ike. One fervent campaigner on his behalf was the vicious anti-Communist Joseph McCarthy. McCarthy's technique was to attack in all directions and, specifically, to challenge the patriotism of many politicians, including George Marshall, the man most responsible for Ike's military career gaining traction during World War II. Ike was outraged, but nevertheless employed a calculated and mild response. It was pragmatic, not heroic.

The real Eisenhower innovation was the use of television. As we've seen, television cameras had been present at the conventions in 1948, but the very limited coverage and the very small number of viewers at that time meant that the television media would not cast a long shadow. The situation in 1952 was quite different; millions of Americans now owned sets. The television networks offered extended broadcast of convention activities, nearly 14 hours each. Some saw this as a good thing. Broadcast journalist and later news anchor Walter Cronkite, for one, thought that broadcasting conventions would convert conventions into the "biggest theatrical drama of all times" and in the process would put weak, dishonest politicians on view for the voters to see. Others worried about this development. Edward R. Murrow, the great CBS newscaster, feared that television would convert conventions (and the campaign) into "carnivals" or, worse, into "horror shows where no hard news was made." The historian Douglas Brinkley captures part of the anxiety this way: "TV was going to place a premium on personality in politicians and being telegenic became almost a prerequisite for seeking national office." The fact that CBS hosted a "how-to-look-good-on-TV" class in 1952 strengthened such anxieties. Soon it would become clear that converting campaigns into televised events would make them vastly more expensive. For Ike, virtually every campaign event, including most major speeches, was televised. As Brinkley notes, "the cameras played perfectly into the Eisenhower-as-folk-hero scenario." Eisenhower hired a television advisor and was comfortable with the medium. Many of the most memorable moments of his campaigns and his presidency would be televised. His Farewell Address of January 1961, seen by 70 million people, is a prime example.

Advertising played a bigger role in 1952 than in any previous campaign. It was perhaps inevitable that Madison Avenue (home of advertising firms) and Pennsylvania Avenue (home of the White House) would work together; "selling" candidates had always been part of the presidential game, and advertising executives had been aiding presidential candidates since the 1920s. In 1952 the 30-second television "spot" (advertisement) made its debut in presidential campaigns. The logic of this development was convincing: a candidate could travel hundreds of miles a day and speak dozens of times but only reach a few thousand people, whereas a prime time spot could reach millions of voters. The Republicans brought in successful advertising executive Rosser Reeves to "sell" the former general. Reeves produced an array of short advertisements and jingles. "I like Ike" became ubiquitous. Eisenhower even took a day off from his busy speaking schedule to film these pieces. The character of American politics was changing, and broadcast executive Sig Mickelson put the change best in the title of his book: *From Whistle Stop to Sound Bite*. The foundation was now laid for actual presidential debates.

Because of its long-term consequences, one of the most important events of the 1952 campaign was Richard Nixon's so-called Checkers speech. Senator Nixon, like many politicians of that era, was not paid enough in salary and allowances to cover all of his office expenses. Being an active politician with national aspirations was costly, and wealthy supporters helped him meet these costs. He was accused of using these funds to supplement his income, though the evidence suggests that he hadn't. But Senator Nixon was vulnerable since he had been complaining bitterly about corruption in Washington. Thus the headline, "Secret Rich Men's Trust Fund Keeps Nixon in Style Far Beyond His Salary." Both Eisenhower and Nixon heard the news on their respective campaign trains. Eisenhower demanded a public accounting. The threat of dropping Nixon was real. The Republican National Committee put up $75,000 for 30 minutes of television time on the evening of September 23. From a studio in Hollywood, Nixon produced what Ambrose calls "one of the great classics of American folklore." Without notes, and with wife Pat visible on camera, Nixon explained his side of the case in the language of a common, plainspoken man. He and his family did not live well, he explained. His wife wore a cloth coat, rather than a fur, and she was not paid out of campaign funds as some political wives were. And finally, their children had been given a little dog, Checkers, as a gift by a supporter. The children loved Checkers, and, as a father, he could not consider returning the dog, even if it was, technically, a political contribution. The program evoked mixed responses. Some viewers were disgusted by the sentimentality; neither Pat nor Ike liked it. But millions of Americans had been moved to tears by the show. Four million letters, telegrams, and phone calls supported Nixon. The power of television in politics was now clear, as was the public's sensibility. And Nixon now saw himself as the master of the new medium.

Stevenson was critical of these tactics. A thoughtful, articulate, and witty man who didn't own a television at the time, he was uncomfortable in this new age. According to historian Eric Burns, Stevenson objected to "selling the presidency like cereal. . . . How can you talk seriously about issues with half minute spots." He struggled with the exacting constraints the medium placed on him: more than once the end of a speech was cut off because it did not fit the time purchased. Knowing he must make some changes, he hired Edward R. Murrow to advise him, and later appeared on "Meet the Press." And in 1956 he participated in the first televised debate in history during a presidential primary election. Still, he could never escape the belief that a campaign needed to be about facts and ideas. This was a mistake. As Eisenhower biographer Jean Edward Smith explains, "in a sense Stevenson appealed to voters' minds, while Eisenhower appealed to their hearts."

Debates in the Information Age (1960–2008)

The 1960 presidential election was typical in one way: while it touched briefly on the issues, it was really an election about the candidates. It was also memorable because it marked another step away from the hopes of the Founders with regard to presidential campaigns and the presidency. The debate between John F. Kennedy and Richard Nixon marked the near-extinction of the idea that presidents stand above politics and parties. It also marked another stage in the triumph of image and impression over ideas in American politics. As Stephen Ambrose puts it, "there were no real differences separating these hot blooded cold warriors so eager for power and so apparently short of principles." Both saw the international confrontation with Communism as their central challenge; both took moderately progressive views on domestic issues, such as civil rights. Both men had shown themselves to be exemplars of modern presidential campaigns, actively engaged in their respective conventions, playing a central role in the choice of the vice presidential nominee, and embracing television as the key mechanism for communicating with the American people. Both men had appeared on the small screen frequently, in speeches, press conferences, and interview programs such as "Meet the Press." As Kennedy himself wrote, in a prescient letter to his future media advisor, "television may be the most important part of the campaign. It may decide the election."

As we have seen, many Americans had longed for debates among presidential candidates, especially in those years when real issues needed to be resolved by the politicians. And on at least a few occasions, something we might call a "debate-at-a-distance" did occur during some campaigns. However, campaign tactics, political ideology, and technology stood in the way of debates becoming a central element of presidential election cycles. Would better-known candidates surrender their advantage by appearing with lesser-known individuals? Would the public accept such open office-seeking? And how could the candidates be brought together so that the nation could see and hear them? Television solved the technical and logistical problem. Forty-six million families owned television sets in 1960. The television networks were eager for debates, eager to enlarge their role in American life and culture, and eager to perform this act of public service. They imagined presidential debates as must-see television—a spectacle not to be missed. A cooperative Congress suspended the provision of the Federal Communications Act of 1934 that required equal time to all candidates for the office, thus permitting a set of debates between the two major party candidates. Kennedy, a relative newcomer to the national arena, pushed hard for televised debates; Nixon, who had served for eight years as vice president, put a lower priority on them. Eisenhower, who knew well the power of television, argued against Nixon's participation. He thought it unnecessary and potentially counterproductive. Public pressure, however, overwhelmed tactical concerns: on July 31, Nixon telegraphed his acceptance of a set of debates to the nation's three television networks and its four radio networks. Ultimately, four debates were agreed to: September 26, October 7, October 13, and October 21. Continuing the tradition of the Lincoln-Douglas debates, each meeting would be in a different city.

Richard Nixon was overconfident. An experienced debater, he had begun his debating career in high school. Later, he debated political opponents as a young politician in California. Most famously, he had also debated Soviet premier Nikita Khrushchev at the American National Exposition in Moscow in 1959 on the issue of whether the Soviet or American systems produced the best homes (the "Kitchen Debate"). This exchange was soon telecast in the United States, significantly enhancing Nixon's reputation. Cameras did not intimidate him in the slightest; he had felt comfortable in front of cameras since the "Checkers" speech. Unfortunately, he did not recognize that television, now more than a decade old, was more of an entertainment medium driven by images than a channel for public information. The public had greater expectations for visual stimulation than in the past. Thus, he gave insufficient attention to how the peculiarities of his appearance (stubble, sweating) or his personality might be perceived. Nixon often projected a formal, perhaps devious seriousness. He did not readily convey warmth, sincerity, or humor. Historian Richard Reeves tells us that Eisenhower's personal secretary observed, "the Vice President sometimes seems like a man who is acting like a nice man rather than being one." Nixon realized too late that he needed to counteract these qualities on screen.

John F. Kennedy was justifiably confident in his abilities, too. He had successfully debated Henry Cabot Lodge, Jr., in his first senatorial campaign in Massachusetts in 1952. More recently, during the presidential primaries, he had debated Hubert Humphrey in West Virginia on television. At the Democratic National Convention in Los Angeles he had debated one of his opponents for the nomination, the much more experienced Lyndon Johnson, in a closed session before the Texas and Massachusetts convention delegations. As Nixon would, so Johnson had underestimated his younger challenger. According to Kennedy biographer Michael O'Brien, Johnson "apparently assumed he could demolish his young opponent in a direct confrontation." Kennedy's appearance and his personality were well-suited to entertainment-oriented television. (He attended CBS's television success seminars back in 1952.) While he was reticent in some respects, in public he was gregarious, confident, articulate, and self-deprecating. On television he appeared polished, serene, and imbued with an Olympian grace. Facing Humphrey, he utilized speechwriter Theodore Sorensen's advice to employ "simple words, short sentences, and calm dignity." Having observed the candidate, *New York Times* journalist James Reston noted that Kennedy was an "articulate participant in the give and take of modern television discussion and debate." Even while Nixon expected to humiliate Kennedy, he did recognize that his opponent "had a very effective ability to project himself on television." Nixon seemed unaware that the game revolved around image rather than facts and ideas.

The first debate, in particular, drew attention to significant differences in the two candidates' approaches to the event. It was to be held in the CBS studios in Chicago. Nixon had refused Eisenhower's offer to loan him his experienced media expert, Robert Montgomery. Having injured his leg early in the campaign and been confined to Walter Reed Army Hospital, Nixon was far from his visual best. He had lost weight and his shirt collar was too large, but he refused to change shirts. He likewise declined professional makeup, and during the debate, under the heat of the lights, perspiration would cause the makeup he did use to run. He wore a light gray suit, which made him visually fade into the set. Some of these mistakes were the result of an ill-informed media strategy, but over-confidence and exhaustion also played a part. He had campaigned hard prior to the telecast, including on the day of the event. In contrast, Kennedy's media expert, J. Leonard Reisch, carefully examined the set in advance. A professional applied light makeup to the tanned and healthy-looking Kennedy. The candidate wore a dark suit, which contrasted agreeably with the set. He was well rested, having had an easy schedule prior to the event, and having spent the day of the debate working on his opening statement and studying his fact cards.

Seventy-five to eighty million people saw this groundbreaking event. Each candidate began with an 8-minute opening statement. Kennedy's call to get the nation moving again, lifted from his Los Angeles acceptance speech, was echoed, rather than contradicted, by Nixon. It was a "me too" moment that failed to convey any disagreement Nixon might have had with Kennedy's general philosophy. Four newsmen, led by Howard K. Smith, then asked questions to the candidates in turn, and the debate ended with closing statements. During the evening, Kennedy had addressed all of his remarks to the television audience, the American people. Nixon, with a more formal debate model in mind, addressed his opponent. This was very different from the typical debate, and certainly different than the Lincoln-Douglas clashes: almost nothing new or spontaneous came out of the encounter. Both men used well-rehearsed lines from earlier separate appearances. Stephen Ambrose argues that the event "was not a debate at all, but rather a press conference." Few serious differences in the two men's political views came to the surface. When polled, few Americans could even remember what had been said.

The consensus of pundits and viewers was that Kennedy had "won" the debate. Only the small, and demographically distinct, radio audience thought differently. Critics who had watched on television noted that Nixon "glowered" and looked "haggard." One sharp-tongued critic suggested that "they've embalmed him before he's even died!" Nixon's effort to be forceful in dealing with Kennedy's arguments backfired with viewers; he was perceived as a bully. As Kennedy biographer Michael O'Brien observes, "image won out over content" in this debate. Another Kennedy biographer, Robert Dallek, goes further: "Kennedy came across as a leader who intended to deal with the nation's greatest problems; Nixon registered on voters as someone trying to gain an advantage over an adversary." Others have noted that Kennedy seemed calm throughout; he looked presidential. Nixon, on the other hand, looked guilty. Nixon had treated the event like a traditional debate competition, rather than what it really was to viewers: a television show. He was critical of his own performance, writing later in his memoir *Six Crises*, "I concentrated too much on substance and not enough on appearance." It is hard to imagine that a long-practicing American politician could make such a mistake. Henry Cabot Lodge, Jr., Nixon's running mate, had a more visceral response in the immediate aftermath of the debate: "That son-of-a-bitch just lost the election."

The pattern established in Chicago varied only slightly in the remaining three debates. Two weeks later, in Washington,

DC, Nixon wore professionally applied makeup and saw to it that the studio was a chilly 64 degrees. The debate focused on America's decline in prestige and power and both men offered aggressive policies to reverse that decline. Only 60 million viewers watched this time. The third debate saw the candidates in different cities, Kennedy in New York and Nixon in Los Angeles, linked through the miracle of electronics. The final debate was held in New York City.

It is not clear what impact, if any, the debates had on the election. It is true that JFK became something of a celebrity; women and girls found him as exciting as they had Frank Sinatra and as they would find the Beatles just a few years later. And it is true that Kennedy's confidence grew as a result and that Nixon's sank; observers noted something like panic among Nixon's backers in the days before the election. However, on the eve of the first debate in September, polls indicated that the candidates were tied—and, on Election Day they were still essentially tied. Perhaps political scientist Samuel Lubell said it best: "My own judgment is that the debates did not bring any basic changes in the voting pattern of the nation." How could it have been otherwise? The debates constituted just one small part of an electoral machine that included, as it had for decades, thousands of tireless party workers, as well as the newer addition of continuous media coverage.

Debates did not immediately become a fixed part of the presidential campaign routine; it would be 16 years before candidates would again face off together in front of cameras. The role of television, however, continued to grow, as the campaigns became more and more candidate-centered. With the 1964 campaign approaching, President Lyndon Johnson faced a choice similar to Nixon's in 1960: should he share a stage with Barry Goldwater and thereby give the lesser-known candidate a boost? He decided not to, and he convinced Congress to restore the legal requirement that if free airtime is being given by the networks, then all candidates must receive it. Similarly, Richard Nixon, when he ran again in 1968 and 1972, opposed giving his opponents public forums for their views. With debates on hiatus, some of the older rituals continued. In 1964, for instance, Johnson's wife, Claudia "Lady Bird" Johnson, traveled across eight southern states on her personal train, the Lady Bird Special. However, most candidates (and their surrogates and spouses) now traveled from speech to speech by plane or helicopter, with the occasional bus ride to keep the "whistle stop" tradition alive. Generating slogans continued to be necessary campaign business. From the beginning of the presidential game in the nineteenth century, catchy slogans have been a part of selling—or attacking—candidates, from "Tippecanoe and Tyler too" to "I like Ike," and this tradition continued. In 1964, for instance, the militant Republican conservative Barry Goldwater brought us the slogan: "In your heart you know he's right." On the other side, his many opponents chanted "In your gut you know he's nuts."

Exaggerations of all sorts, charges of moral depravity, and dark accusations about a candidate's patriotism appeared. Such things were a perennial part of the game. But television had now become a part of the tradition as well, with candidates now appearing in a hybrid role: the politician/celebrity. Early media master Richard Nixon realized that his face left television viewers cold, but he learned that images of his daughters, and even his future son-in-law, David Eisenhower, prompted much warmer feelings. And warm feelings brought votes. He also recognized the importance of complete scripting for major television events, such as the Republican

National Convention in 1976. Gerald Ford was generally ineffective on television, but nevertheless he appeared in a guest spot on *Saturday Night Live*. Much later Bill Clinton would play "Heartbreak Hotel" on a saxophone on the *Arsenio Hall Show*, while later he and wife Hillary would discuss their often-troubled marriage on *60 Minutes*. In 1992 the third-party candidate, H. Ross Perot announced his candidacy on CNN's *Larry King Live* and then, after dropping out briefly, re-announced there. Historian Timothy Naftali suggests that "the Perot presidential campaign was a creation of the media." Perhaps the clearest example of television's dominance was the White House of Ronald Reagan. There, nearly every event was scripted for television and the "actor-in-chief" was given a daily shooting script and cue cards. (Reagan was particularly suited for this role, since he was a former Hollywood actor.) Presidential candidates and presidents were increasingly a part of the media-driven celebrity culture; their ultimate success depended on their comfort in, and mastery of, that world. Presidents and presidential aspirants could no longer be above or outside of the world of mass media—they were enmeshed in it.

Presidential debates returned in 1976, the bicentennial year, and they have become a fixed part of the presidential election game. But the question of sponsorship posed a difficult problem: who would establish formats, choose moderators, and pick locations? The media had organized the Kennedy-Nixon meeting, but in 1976 the debate returned, organized by the non-partisan League of Women Voters. The League produced the debates in 1976, 1980, and 1984. It proved to be too great—and too controversial—a task for that organization, however. In 1987 the issue of sponsorship was resolved with the formation of the Commission on Presidential Debates.

This non-partisan, non-profit organization has handled the task every four years ever since. But questions remained: how many debates should there be? Nixon and Kennedy had met four times. Was that the right number? How many candidates should be invited? Should the nominees for vice president debate? (In 1976 they did for the first time.) And what should the format be? What would best serve the voters? The Great Debate of 1960 was, according to some, an elaborate news conference, where previously used slogans and talking points were recycled. Would long speeches, as Lincoln and Douglas had delivered, be better? Would the format of academic debate be better? Or, given the medium, would some sort of judged competition be best: "Dancing with the Candidates"? What has appeared after 1976 has been a series of public confrontations, which, because they take place in front of the television cameras, usually generate more theater than intellectual or policy substance. They have become a subset of the massive media effort that constitutes the modern version of the presidential game. Their impact on the 24-hour news cycle and on popular culture has sometimes been significant, but their impact on elections seems limited—just as in 1960.

In 1976 President Gerald Ford initiated a set of three debates with his popular opponent, Jimmy Carter. Ford, known for his halting, plodding, uninspiring efforts at speech making, wanted to demonstrate his presidential qualities and his command of facts at the expense of his less experienced opponent. In this sense, Ford was destined to repeat Nixon's mistake in 1960. As the campaign opened, Ford was thirty points behind in the polls. Approximately 100 million people saw the re-inauguration of the debate tradition on September 23. The second debate, on October 6, was also seen by a very large audience. There, Ford made a major error. He was asked about the impact of the Nixon-Ford policy of detente with the Soviet Union; many conservatives, including his opponent in the primaries, Ronald Reagan, argued that *detente* abandoned nations like Poland to communist control. Ford's response shocked nearly everyone. He asserted that, "[t]here is no Soviet domination of Eastern Europe," adding that the nations of that region don't consider themselves dominated. According to even friendly observers, these remarks were careless and unwise. Ford spent the last month of the campaign clarifying and correcting what he had said. Yet as glaring as this public gaffe was, its impact on the election was minimal: in the last poll before the election the thirty-point Carter lead had become a one-point Ford lead. The impact of the first vice presidential debate seems equally uncertain. Republican Bob Dole's efforts at a highly partisan confrontation backfired and the Democrat Walter Mondale was deemed the winner. Although the Ford/Dole team lost that election, it was one of the closest of the century. Ford's biographer notes that his chances of reelection were crippled by the poor state of the economy and by the long, bruising battle with Ronald Reagan for the Republican nomination. The debates had little impact.

The election of 1980 pitted Jimmy Carter against Ronald Reagan and again showed the dominance of showmanship over discussion of serious issues in the television-debate format. When elected in 1976 Carter had been seen as bright, engaging, and media savvy; he knew how to manipulate images and symbols. He had learned the value of wearing jeans at public appearances. Much of the media cooperated in portraying him as a Georgian JFK: young, bright, photogenic, and authentic. However, by 1980, crises in Afghanistan and Iran had exhausted him and turned the media hostile. According to his biographer Julian Zelizer, he had withdrawn from debates in the primaries, arguing that "national unity . . . would be jeopardized by participating in partisan events." He was perceived as nasty and mean. In the second debate he appeared tense and sounded testy as he displayed his policy expertise. Unlike four years earlier, he now worked on the assumption that "the issues are more important than performance." In Ronald Reagan, he faced a relaxed, smiling, confident opponent, much like Kennedy in 1960. Reagan was little interested in policy details. As the biographer Jules Tygiel, author of *Ronald Reagan and the Triumph of Conservatism*, notes, "Reagan reigned as one of the nation's most gifted storytellers, but the tales he conveyed were often riddled with factual errors or flatly untrue." In the debate, Carter launched into a fact-filled attack on one of Reagan's positions, phrased in biting language. It was as though he was lecturing a not-so-bright student in front of the entire nation. However, the student got the upper hand. The cameras caught Reagan chuckling during Carter's dissertation. When he got the microphone, he said, "There you go again." The president's command of facts was belittled and his temperament gently mocked. Reagan won. As had been the case in 1960, the appearance of confidence and good humor trumps nearly everything else in our presidential debates.

In 1984 the aging, but still popular, Ronald Reagan stood for reelection. Walter Mondale, Carter's vice president, opposed him. There were no significant issues; the nation was prosperous and at peace. Mondale was far behind in the polls. There were just two debates, but they clearly illustrated the central role of appearance, image, and theatrical flair in these events. In the first debate the 73-year-old Reagan lacked his usual charm and magic; he seemed unfocused, giving rise to mutterings about his capacity to manage a second term.

His lead in the polls slipped. However, for the second debate the rested and better-briefed old actor pleased the audience with a classic *coup de theatre*. Knowing that the nation was watching for evidence of mental competence, he launched a pre-emptive strike: "I will not make age an issue in this campaign. I am not going to exploit, for political purposes, my opponent's youth and inexperience." The audience erupted in laughter, as did Mondale himself. Game over.

In 1988 Reagan left the political stage and lesser actors occupied it. George H. W. Bush was the Republican candidate. He had been a Reagan critic when he was a competitor for the nomination in 1980, but had gone on to be a loyal vice president. His Democratic opponent was Governor Michael Dukakis of Massachusetts. The campaign ranks high in the pantheon of vicious, bitter, divisive elections. Republicans portrayed Dukakis as "soft on crime," and introduced the image of a murderous paroled criminal, Willy Horton, as a case study in the dangers of being too generous to criminals. There were just two debates; neither was very exciting, because neither man had Reagan's flair. The only spark generated in the presidential debates occurred when Dukakis, who focused on policy, was asked: "Governor, if Kitty Dukakis (his wife) were raped and murdered, would you favor an irrevocable death penalty for the killer?" His response maintaining his opposition to the death penalty was detached and passionless. It left people cold. The real excitement was in the vice presidential debate. Dan Quayle, a young senator from Indiana, was Bush's choice; Dukakis tapped the seasoned senator Lloyd Bentsen from Texas as his running mate. In response to suggestions that he was unprepared for the vice presidency, Quayle had been comparing himself to the youthful—and, of course, much revered—John F. Kennedy. Bentsen was determined to destroy that image in a theatrical scene of his own. When Quayle offered the comparison in debate, Bentsen rebutted it in a carefully prepared but spontaneous-sounding reply: "Senator, I served with Jack Kennedy. I knew Jack Kennedy. Jack Kennedy was a friend of mine. Senator, you are no Jack Kennedy." It was the most memorable — and most quoted — line in the three debates, but its impact on the outcome is hard to determine.

The next four election cycles produced some format innovations to the emerging debate tradition, but little substance or drama. In 1992 there were three candidates, Republican George H. W. Bush, Democrat Bill Clinton, and the independent candidate, businessman H. Ross Perot. According to Timothy Naftali, the Bush camp insisted that Perot be include in the debates; they made the classic error of underestimating him, assuming that he was "too small and too shifty to be president," and that his weaknesses would be readily apparent on television. However, in general, Perot held his own. His height became an issue in the third debate when he refused to sit on the stool provided because his feet would not touch the ground. He stood awkwardly during the telecast. The innovation that appeared in 1992 was the "town hall" debate format, where pre-screened audience members, rather than reporters, asked the questions. Bill Clinton, generally more relaxed in the give-and-take of such a setting, did well, while Bush stumbled. Mishearing a question from the audience, he responded, "I'm not sure I get it." This phrase seemed to confirm the argument of his opponents that he was out of touch with the nation. However, neither the awkward images of short candidates or awkward phrases taken out of context decided the election; the state of the economy did. As the Clinton campaign maintained, "It's the economy, stupid."

In 1996 there were just two debates, the second of which was in the town hall format. The politically weakened Perot did not run this time. The textbook *Presidential Elections* assesses the 1996 debates this way: they "produced few memorable moments, and appeared to change little in the race." The two debates in the 2000 election cycle pitted a disciplined, knowledgeable Al Gore, Clinton's vice president, against the less articulate, less informed George W. Bush, governor of Texas. Gore repeated a classic error: he was aggressive, dismissive, and sometimes rude; he obsessively mentioned that he would put Social Security and Medicare in a "lockbox" to protect them from mean-spirited entitlement cutters. He succeeded in making Bush seem more likable. Gore's staff prescribed a dose of media administered humility: watching a parody of his debate performance on *Saturday Night Live*. In terms of affecting the election outcome, the debates were a wash. Finally, in 2004, John Kerry, the Democratic challenger, debated George Bush three times, with the second debate being the town hall event. In the first event, Bush seemed impatient, uneasy, and inarticulate; Kerry won, according to media observers. The remaining two were more even. In any case, while Kerry gained slightly on Bush in the polls after the first debate, the outcome was still a significant defeat.

The most recent debates in 2008 continued to present more public entertainment than a source of political enlightenment. Three debates were scheduled for senators Barack Obama and John McCain, the second meeting in a town hall format. McCain's strategy was to reveal to the American people that Obama was weak, naive, and not competent enough to be president. He insisted repeatedly that his opponent "doesn't seem to understand." Even with his efforts to say this politely, it largely backfired. By and large, the presidential debates were, in the words of the authors of *Presidential Elections*, largely "uneventful." According to most observers, including most independent voters, Obama won the debates. In the October 2 vice presidential debate, there was a great deal of interest in seeing Alaska governor Sarah Palin debate Vice President Joe Biden; the confluence of gender, style, and experience had pundits excited. The outcome was less memorable than hoped for. As happened so often in the past, the debates in 2008 were more theatrical than informational. Or, as the authors of *Presidential Elections* note, "as usual, the 2008 debates failed to produce any developments important enough to significantly affect the trajectory of the campaign." Must this be so?

At the beginning of the American presidency, our chief executives sought to stay above politics, above partisanship, to be presidents of all the people. They isolated themselves from elections and allowed the parties to take on the dirty work of campaigning. Presidential elections, like baseball, became a great national game. Over time and as part of the great democratic revolution, candidates, rather than parties, became the stars of these great contests. The image of presidents as tribunes, protectors of the public interest, gave way to the image of presidents as leaders of interest groups. Actively and publicly seeking office became legitimate. Today, candidates raise far more money than parties do; the election, after all, is about them. Debates between candidates are more valuable than ever. We often portray our presidential elections as debates, maybe even great debates. However, debates about principles until recently did not mean a debate between persons. Tradition and logistics were against real debates. How could any joint appearance reach enough voters to justify them? Radio and television provided the solution: candidates could be heard by millions simultaneously. Thus we had the Great Debates of 1960. Those four confrontations between Nixon and Kennedy established a couple of key elements of the tradition: they involved more theater than content and their impact was ultimately unclear. The 1960 confrontations showed the importance of appearance and demeanor; acting ability was valuable. But even the best performance, it became clear, has a limited hold on our memories or our minds; our years-long, 24/7, media-saturated election campaigns drown us in images, impressions, and phrases. The debates, therefore, boil down to being single episodes of a popular show in a lengthy television season.

So the question becomes: can we make these now-traditional events richer in content and more helpful as a mechanism for choosing a president? Perhaps it is simply a matter of format: would a wider variety of moderators or a broader pool of questions solve the problem? Perhaps something more radical is needed. Presidential elections, as we have seen, have since the 1830s been a colorful, entertaining game more notable for its slogans than for its discussion of issues. Can the presidential debates become models for the serious, thoughtful discussion of public issues? Will social media help? Can it take us beyond image and entertainment to the solutions to the pressing issues of our times? Perhaps these are questions for the younger generation.

Discussion Questions

1. Explain why contemporary debates between presidential candidates would have been "shocking" to the Founding Fathers.

2. Describe the relationship between the presidential candidates and their political parties in the early U.S. presidential campaigns.
3. To what extent are candidates today too ideologically tied to one party to be able to govern in the interests of the nation as a whole? Justify your position.
4. To what extent did the increasing ease of travel and communication in the nineteenth century affect the nature of the presidential campaigns?
5. Compare and contrast the tactics employed in the early presidential campaigns with campaign strategies today.
6. Imagine what a modern presidential campaign would look like if candidates remained "above politics." In your opinion, would the outcomes for American citizens be improved if politicians took this hands-off approach?
7. In the four-way presidential campaign of 1912, explore the role of performance in the campaign speeches of Wilson and Roosevelt. To what extent did this affect the outcome of the election?
8. Explore the ways in which "appearance of confidence and good humor" is more important than policy expertise in presidential debates. Give historic examples.
9. Should candidates' personal lives be discussed in the debates?
10. According to the author, do the debates affect the outcome of the election? Either way, do you think the debates are useful? How so?
11. If you were moderating a presidential debate, what question would you ask the candidates? Why?
12. Present your ideas for making presidential debates more engaging and impactful on the outcome of the elections.

Bibliography

Ambrose, Stephen E. *Nixon*. 3 vols. New York: Simon & Schuster, 1987–91. Ambrose's extensive biography of Nixon offers a deep examination of this complex historical figure. Also see Richard Reeves's *President Nixon*.

Ambrose, Stephen E. *Eisenhower: Soldier and President*. New York: Simon & Schuster, 1990. Ambrose's detailed biography of Eisenhower highlights his position as a reluctant politician during the 1952 campaign.

Bailyn, Bernard. *The Ideological Origins of the American Revolution*. Cambridge, MA: Belknap Press of Harvard University Press, 1992. This important study of the revolutionary generation helped illuminate the philosophy of the Founders for contemporary historians.

Boller, Paul F. *Presidential Campaigns: From George Washington to George W. Bush*. New York: Oxford University Press, 1996. Boller's brief accounts of each campaign include valuable and interesting details and anecdotes. For a more academic account, see Polsby et al.'s *Presidential Elections*.

Brinkley, Douglas. *Cronkite*. New York: Harper, 2012. This biography of news anchor Walter Cronkite — once known as "the most trusted man in America" — gives insight into the debates from the perspective of the media. Also see Eric Burns's *Invasion of the Mind Snatchers*.

Burns, Eric. *Invasion of the Mind Snatchers: Television's Conquest of America in the Fifties*. Philadelphia: Temple University Press, 2010. Television's transformation of American society set the stage for the modern presidential debates.

Burns, James MacGregor. *Roosevelt: The Lion and the Fox*. New York: Harcourt Brace Jovanovich, 1984. The first biography of Franklin Delano Roosevelt, this work presents a comprehensive account of FDR's political life until 1940.

Burns, James MacGregor. *Roosevelt: Soldier of Freedom, 1940–1945*. New York: Harcourt Brace Jovanovich, 1970. Picking up where *The Lion and the Fox* leaves off, this volume covers Roosevelt's war years. It is dense, but insightful.

Chance, James. *1912: Wilson, Roosevelt, Taft, and Debs — The Election that Changed the Country*. New York: Simon & Schuster, 2005. Chance tells the tale of this transformative election in an engaging manner.

Cooper, John Milton, Jr. *The Warrior and the Priest: Woodrow Wilson and Theodore Roosevelt*. Cambridge: Belknap Press of Harvard University Press, 1985. This is a useful guide for studying the great campaign of 1912 and understanding the differences between these two candidates.

Dallek, Robert. *An Unfinished Life: John F. Kennedy, 1917–1963*. New York: Back Bay Books, 2004. This recent biography of JFK reveals much about the president's personal struggles, examining both the politics and the psychology of this celebrated politician. Also see Michael O'Brien's *John F. Kennedy*.

Dean, John W. *Warren G. Harding: The 29th President, 1921–1923*. The American Presidents Series. New York: Times Books, 2004. Dean's biography offers a quirky but interesting tale of this presidency.

Donaldson, Gary A. *The First Modern Campaign: Kennedy, Nixon, and the Election of 1960*. Lanham, MD: Rowman & Littlefield, 2007. Donaldson provides an engaging guide to the first election where presidential candidates debated face-to-face. Also see Theodore White's *The Making of the President*.

Donovan, Robert. *Conflict and Crisis: The Presidency of Harry S. Truman, 1945–1948*. New York: Norton, 1977. The best biography that focuses on Truman's presidency, including the famous 1948 election against Thomas Dewey.

Hamilton, Alexander, James Madison, and John Jay. *The Federalist Papers*. Charleston, SC: Tribeca Books, 2011. The classic defense of the new constitutional government. Writing under the pseudonym "Publius," Hamilton, Madison, and Jay argued in favor of ratifying the Constitution.

Jefferson, Thomas. *The Portable Thomas Jefferson*. Edited by Merrill D. Peterson. New York: Viking Press, 1975. This is an expansive collection of Jefferson's writings.

Kazin, Michael. *A Godly Hero*. New York: Alfred A. Knopf, 2007. This biography of William Jennings Bryan unlocks many mysteries about the man and the great culture wars that began with the Populist uprising of the late-nineteenth century and that continue today.

Ketcham, Ralph. *Presidents Above Party: The First American Presidency, 1789–1829*. Chapel Hill: University of North Carolina Press, 1987. Ketcham explains the role of the early presidents in their own campaigns.

Naftali, Timothy. *George H.W. Bush: The 41st President*. The American Presidents Series. New York: Macmillan, 2007. This entry in the American Presidents Series gives insight into the 1988 and 1992 debates. For the full series, see Wilentz and Schlesinger.

Nixon, Richard. *Six Crises*. New York: Simon & Schuster, 1990. Nixon's memoir recounts the 1960 presidential debates and the Checkers speech.

Malone, Dumas. *Jefferson and His Time*. 6 vols. Boston: Little, Brown, 1948–81. This monumental biography includes detailed accounts of every stage of Jefferson's political life.

McCormick, Richard P. *The Presidential Game: The Origins of American Presidential Politics.* New York: Oxford University Press, 1982. McCormick defines the rules of the "Presidential Game" in the early American Republic and explains how they still affect presidential elections. Also see Mark Summers's *The Party Game.*

Newton, Jim. *Eisenhower: The White House Years.* New York: Doubleday, 2011. Newton's work covers Eisenhower's presidency, but also provides useful context from his pre-presidency years. Also see Jean Edward Smith's *Eisenhower in War and Peace.*

Oates, Stephen B. *With Malice Toward None: The Life of Abraham Lincoln.* New York: Harper & Row, 1997. This humanizing biography examines Lincoln's character and illustrates how he approached the difficult issues of his day.

O'Brien, Michael. *John F. Kennedy: A Biography.* New York: Thomas Dunne Books, 2005. This is one of the more extensive biographies on Kennedy. Also see Robert Dallek's *An Unfinished Life.*

Peterson, Merrill. *Thomas Jefferson and the New Nation: A Biography.* New York: Oxford University Press, 1970. Peterson sets the standard for biographies of Jefferson. It may lack criticism of the Founder, but this work successfully addresses his full life in one volume.

Polsby, Nelson W., Aaron Wildavsky, Steven E. Schier, and David Hopkins. *Presidential Elections: Strategies and Structures of American Politics.* Lanham, MD: Rowman & Littlefield, 2012. The authors take an academic approach to studying presidential elections. For a more accessible book, see Paul Boller's *Presidential Campaigns.*

Reeves, Richard. *President Nixon: Alone in the White House.* New York: Simon & Schuster, 2001. Reeves captures the character of this embattled president better than any other biographer. Also see Stephen Ambrose's *Nixon*.

Shroeder, Alan. *Presidential Debates: Fifty Years of High-Risk TV*, 2nd ed. New York: Columbia University Press, 2008. This book carries the debate story into the present, with a particular focus on the technical issues.

Smith, Jean Edward. *Eisenhower in War and Peace.* New York: Random House, 2012. Smith, an experienced presidential biographer, gives an in-depth and balanced account of Eisenhower's record. Also see Jim Newton's *Eisenhower*.

Summers, Mark. *Party Games: Getting, Keeping, and Using Power in Gilded Age Politics*. Chapel Hill: University of North Carolina Press, 2004. Summers looks at late-nineteenth-century American politics through an institutional lens, helping clarify the impact that candidates during that time had on the history of presidential elections.

Tocqueville, Alexis de. *Democracy in America.* New York: Library of America, 2004. This seminal work is the starting point for any serious study of American society, culture, or politics.

Tygiel, Jules. *Ronald Reagan and the Triumph of American Conservatism.* New York: Longman, 2004. A straightforward biography that discusses the Great Communicator's techniques in dealing with the media.

White, Theodore H. *The Making of the President, 1960.* Cutchogue, NY: Buccaneer Books, 1999. This famous work of political journalism provides a great look at the 1960 election between Kennedy and Nixon. Also see Gary Donaldson's *The First Modern Campaign*.

Wilentz, Sean and Arthur Schlesinger, Jr., eds. *The American Presidents.* 38 vols. New York: Times Books, 2003–09. The history-minded will be drawn to this comprehensive and nearly complete series. These short volumes have been written by scholars, journalists, and even the occasional politician.

Zelizer, Julian E. *Jimmy Carter*. New York: Times Books, 2010. This entry in the American Presidents Series serves as a critical but balanced account of the Carter presidency. For the full series, see Wilentz and Schlesinger.

DOMESTIC POLICY

Education

Ted Mateoc

Ensuring that all citizens have access to a decent education is one of the primary duties of a modern government. Primary and secondary education are crucial for successful socialization, the acquiring of civic values, and the development of crucial life skills ranging from literacy to multiplication to understanding the complexities of the world. Mastering a field of knowledge through post-secondary education allows individuals to raise their living standards and their socio-economic positions in society. It also helps ensure continual innovation. In the United States, approximately 90 percent of students from pre-kindergarten through grade 8 attend public schools, placing the burden for a decent education on the government.[1]

President George W. Bush reformed the modern education system with the passage of the No Child Left Behind (NCLB) Act of 2001, which attempted to use standardized testing and teacher evaluation to measure and increase the quality of primary and secondary education American students receive. Standards for tests are set at the state level while the federal

---

1. U.S. Census Bureau, "Statistical Abstract of the United States: 2012," accessed July 31, 2012, http://www.census.gov/compendia/statab/2012/tables/12s0219.pdf.

government provides funding to help offset costs incurred by state budgets. On a practical level, NCLB is the standard for education reform, and either President Barack Obama or Governor Mitt Romney will have to work within the provisions of the law after the 2012 election. Mr. Romney was governor of Massachusetts after Congress passed NCLB, while President Obama took office after the law's passage.

One of the key political debates about education centers on the idea of student choice. Both Mr. Obama and Mr. Romney support charter schools and thus a certain degree of increased student choice, as charter schools are publicly funded schools that are allowed a certain degree of independence from academic regulations in return for producing a higher level of academic achievement. However, Mr. Romney additionally supports school vouchers while Mr. Obama does not. School vouchers (or education vouchers) are certificates issued by the government that parents can use to be reimbursed for private tuition costs. Mr. Romney argues that such a system would improve student choice and thus indirectly improve school accountability, as the underperforming schools would be used by fewer students. Mr. Obama opposes the use of such vouchers, arguing that the policy hollows out the public education system because less money would go toward public schools if students opted out of them.

While in office, President Obama has instituted Race to the Top, a system of federal grants designed to reward schools that meet certain educational benchmarks and reforms. These grants are designed to ensure that states set education policy that is amenable to the federal government. Increased government spending on education was an Obama campaign plank in 2008, as then-senator Obama explained that he supported a certain type of merit pay based on a teacher's dedication to the profession, including demonstrated professional development, rather than year-by-year results.[2] Merit pay is an idea built into NCLB that pays teachers according to how well their students perform on certain standardized tests. Mr. Romney is a supporter of the president's policies on merit pay and school choice, describing Obama's steps as "positive."[3]

Issues surrounding higher education differ greatly from those related to primary and secondary education. The quality and cost of higher education in the United States vary widely. Unlike in many developed nations, where higher education is provided by the national government, American higher education is provided by private institutions as well as by public institutions run by the states. Post-secondary education is not compulsory, and citizens who wish to go to college must find a way to pay their own way, either at public schools or more expensive private colleges. Students may receive grants (scholarships that do not have to be paid back) or loans to pay for their education. Even with these options, however, a good college education is prohibitively expensive for many. The average student with loans graduates almost $25,000 in debt, which adds up to $902 billion of student loan debt nationwide.[4] The federal government now lends 88 percent of the money for student loans, with $795 billion lent, so the

---

2. "Transcript: Barack Obama on 'FOX News Sunday,'" Fox News, April 28, 2008, accessed July 31, 2012, http://www.foxnews.com/story/0,2933,352785,00. html.

3. Mike Allen, "Some Supercommittee Members Left Town in Closing Days," *Politico*, November 22, 2011, accessed July 31, 2012, http://www.politico. com/playbook/1111/playbook1611.html.

4. "Student Loan Debt History," Federal Reserve Bank of New York, accessed July 27, 2012, http://www.newyorkfed.org/studentloandebt/.

next president may face the responsibility of addressing the size of student loan debt.

President Obama has prioritized the issue of student loans. In 2010, he advocated for and signed student loan reform meant to expand college access to millions of Americans. This law expanded the role of the federal government in administering loans, provided funds to expand Pell Grants, which go to students in great financial need, and made it easier for former students to pay back their loans, by allowing them to cap their repayment rate at 10 percent of their income.[5] In the summer of 2012, he supported a measure that froze interest rates, thus preventing student loan rates from doubling, as they would have if Congress had not acted.

If elected, Mr. Romney would try to reverse Mr. Obama's 2010 reform. "A Romney administration will embrace a private-sector role in providing information, financing and education itself, working with effective businesses to support the goals of students and their families," according to Mr. Romney's education-policy platform.[6]

Mr. Romney has also stated that America should place more emphasis on higher education, especially post-graduate degrees. He feels that the emphasis on higher education after World War II helped propel American to its current position in the world economy and that in order for America to remain competitive we must remain committed to emphasizing higher

---

5. Peter Baker and David M. Herszenhorn, "Obama Signs Overhaul of Student Loan Program," March 30, 2010, accessed August 14, 2012, http://www.nytimes.com/2010/03/31/us/politics/31obama.html.

6. Cory Brown, "Candidates Clash Over 2010 Student-Loan Reform Act," *Washington Times*, July 25, 2012, accessed July 31, 2012, http://www.washingtontimes.com/news/2012/jul/25/candidates-clash-over-2010-student-loan-reform-act/.

education, focusing on engineering, computer science, and technology. In 2010, he wrote, "[China and India] graduate more than two times the number of students in these fields as we do. . . . This is a stunning reversal of global preeminence in the priority attached to the highest level of educational attainment."[7]

President Obama, like Mr. Romney, is concerned about increasing the number of workers in the high-tech sector to fulfill a seriously growing need by employers. If reelected, Mr. Obama will continue to push an $8 billion program to train community college students for high-growth industries and provide financial incentives to programs that ensured their trainees find work.[8]

Discussion Questions

1. Compare and contrast the candidates' views on school vouchers.
2. What is the average debt of a college graduate with student loans?
3. Is Governor Romney's opposition to publicly funding higher education at odds with his emphasis on the importance of education for maintaining America's global competitiveness? Explain your position.
4. Describe President Obama's Race to the Top education policy.

---

7. Mitt Romney, *No Apology: The Case for American Greatness* (New York: St. Martin's Press, 2010).

8. Associated Press Business Staff, "Obama Takes Tougher Stance on Higher Education," Cleveland.com, February 20, 2012, accessed July 31, 2012, http://www.cleveland.com/business/index.ssf/2012/02/obama_takes_tougher_stance_on.html.

5. How do Governor Romney and President Obama propose to achieve a balance between the need for students to be able to choose to attend high performing institutions with the need to improve the public education system overall?

Environment

David Katz

After China, the United States is the largest emitter of carbon dioxide, which is the primary contributor to climate change. Of large countries only Australia pollutes more per capita. In recent years, the cost of oil—the primary source of carbon emissions—has been at an all-time high. Climate change and efforts to extract resources for energy in the United States have hurt local ecosystems, raising strong environmental concerns. But solving these problems is neither cheap nor easy. Businesses remain strongly resistant to regulations or taxes on carbon emissions and other types of pollution, and there are economic benefits to drilling at home, including the relatively cheap extraction of resources and the jobs created by domestic projects. For these reasons, recent Republican presidents, starting with Ronald Reagan in 1980, have sought to frame business and the environment as opposing interests, and have tended to favor business in that battle. Democratic presidents, on the other hand, have usually sought solutions that benefit both the environment and business, and have been more willing to regulate business in the interest of environmental protection.

President George W. Bush took more action on this issue than any president in the last three decades, supporting strongly pro-business policies, such as removing environmental regulations and launching a program to examine if humans really have an impact on climate change.[1] In this context, then-senator Barack Obama was elected as a generally pro-environment president, promising to support diverse solutions to address climate change.

President Barack Obama and Governor Mitt Romney have different views on America's energy future, but both candidates have a track record of bolstering the green sector. For Mr. Obama, such efforts include job creation and diminishing dependency on foreign oil by funding alternative energy industries. As governor of Massachusetts, Mr. Romney helped spark a green revolution by promoting green-energy subsidies, where the government gives money to companies that develop solar, wind, and other renewable energy resources.

Mr. Romney's energy platform reflects the conservative attitude evident in the policy of past Republican presidents, an approach best described as "drill, baby, drill" (a slogan popularized by 2008 Republican vice-presidential candidate Sarah Palin). Andrea Saul, one of Mr. Romney's spokespersons, has said, "Governor Romney will permit drilling wherever it can be done safely, taking into account local concerns."[2] Such a policy not only implies drilling for oil but also for natural gas through hydraulic fracturing and the extraction of tar sands.

---

1. Norman J. Vig, "Presidential Leadership and the Environment," in *Environmental Policy: New Directions for the Twenty-First Century*, 3rd ed., ed. Norman J. Vig and Michael E. Kraft (Washington, D.C.: Congressional Quarterly Press, 2006), 115–117.

2. Steven Mufson and Juliet Eilperin, "Romney Energy Plan Shows Candidate's Changing Views, Draws Questions on Job Claims," *Washington Post*, June 8, 2012, accessed July 31, 2012, http://www.washingtonpost.com/business/economy/romney-energy-plan-shows-changing-views-draws-questions-about-job-claims/2012/06/08/gJQAnPANOV_story.html.

With natural gas in abundance across the United States, this approach has earned wide popular support, as it could supply cheap energy and create jobs.

In contrast, Mr. Obama's position, while not the stark opposite some liberals have hoped for, calls for America's energy future to rest on a much more diverse portfolio. His energy policy allows for offshore drilling and "clean" coal combustion to continue, while also encouraging continued growth in the renewable sector. Over the past year, the president has given public support to clean energy tax incentives sent before Congress that would benefit both wind and solar energy. Mr. Obama has also reversed much of Mr. Bush's interior policy, such as by setting higher fuel-efficiency standards for cars and ordering an end to uranium extraction in mines near the Grand Canyon.[3]

Because the coal, oil, and gas industries have a strong business structure in the United States, Republicans commonly base their energy policy on its support. In contrast, the clean energy sector, as a young industry, has experienced a turbulent pattern of growth and instability over the last decade, which has scared potential investors. If Romney and the Republican Party win in November, oil and gas will continue to run the American energy marketplace, maintaining the status quo of unfavorable market conditions for renewable energy investment. If Obama is reelected, however, it is believed that his administration will create a federal renewable portfolio standard—that is, a regulation that requires increased production of renewable energy sources

---

3. Erin Kelly, "Obama Reversing Bush's Environmental Policies," *AZ Central*, April 15, 2010, accessed July 31, 2012, http://www.azcentral.com/news/art icles/2010/04/15/20100415obama-reverses-bush-environmental-policies. html.

like wind, solar, biomass, and geothermal– that would spur growth in the clean energy sector. With the upcoming election, the country's course of action on energy priorities will be set for years to come.

Discussion Questions

1. How does America's carbon footprint compare with other nations?
2. Summarize how Republican and Democratic presidents have traditionally approached the issue of environmental protection.
3. To what extent will the outcome of the 2012 election affect America's long-term energy future?
4. In your opinion, does President Obama go far enough in protecting the environment and ensuring a sustainable energy future for the United States?
5. Identify the reasons why Governor Romney's national energy agenda has earned him "wide popular support" with voters.

Marriage Equality

Christine Seo

A CNN poll released on June 6, 2012, found that 54 percent of Americans believe same-sex marriage should be legal.[1] Those who oppose same-sex marriage often do so because of religious or other traditions that define marriage as a union between a man and a woman. Same-sex marriage supporters believe that marriage for everybody is a civil right, or that it is not the role of the government to dictate who marries and who does not. In contrast, many other citizens believe that the government should not grant marriages to anybody, leaving the responsibility to churches and social institutions.

Currently, marriage laws are administered by the individual states, with some states allowing same-sex marriage, some allowing civil unions—which provide benefits similar to marriage without using the term—and the majority allowing neither. On the federal level, Congress passed the Defense of Marriage Act in 1996, which then-president Bill Clinton signed into law. This law defines marriage as a union between a man and a woman, though its legal status is currently in question

---

1. "Poll: More Americans Favor Same-Sex Marriage," *CNN*, Political Ticker, April 19, 2011, accessed August 14, 2012, http://politicalticker.blogs.cnn.com/2011/04/19/poll-more-americans-favor-same-sex-marriage/.

because of court challenges claiming that it is unconstitutional. Similarly, a president could advocate for and potentially sign a law making same-sex marriage legal throughout the United States, but its constitutionality would also be in question until a Supreme Court decision on the issue.

According to the advocacy organization Freedom to Marry, same-sex marriage is currently legal in the District of Columbia and six states: Connecticut, Iowa, Massachusetts, New Hampshire, New York, and Vermont. Maryland, New Jersey, and Washington have passed same-sex marriage bills that are not yet in effect. Nine states have broad domestic partnerships or civil unions: California, Delaware, Hawaii, Illinois, Nevada, New Jersey, Oregon, Rhode Island, and Washington. Four states have limited domestic partnerships: Colorado, Maine, Maryland, and Wisconsin. The remaining 31 states do not allow domestic partnerships for same-sex couples.

President Barack Obama became the most pro-gay rights presidential candidate in history when he announced during his 2008 campaign that he was supportive of the gay community by supporting civil unions and calling on American citizens to embrace their gay and lesbian neighbors.[2] However, Obama qualified his view at the time by saying he held internal conflicts with regard to reconciling his support of the gay, lesbian, bisexual, transgender, and queer community with his Christian beliefs. On July 19, 2011, the Obama administration announced its support for a bill submitted by Senator Dianne Feinstein, Democrat of California, to repeal the Defense of Marriage Act (DOMA). The Obama administration has already

---

2. Andrew Jacobs, "For Gay Democrats, a Primary Where Rights Are Not an Issue, This Time," *New York Times*, January 28, 2008, accessed August 14, 2012, http://www.nytimes.com/2008/01/28/us/politics/28gay.html.

dropped its legal defense of DOMA amid the current Justice Department's doubts as to its constitutionality. As part of his 2012 presidential campaign, on May 9, 2012, Mr. Obama endorsed same sex marriage, explaining his unqualified decision with the statement, "I want everyone treated fairly in this country. We have never gone wrong when we've extended rights and responsibilities to everybody."[3]

Republican presidential candidate Mitt Romney has consistently maintained his stance against same-sex marriage throughout his political career of nearly twenty years. When the Massachusetts Supreme Court decided in 2003 that same-sex marriage is protected in the Massachusetts constitution, Romney declared, "I agree with 3,000 years of recorded history. I disagree with the Supreme Judicial Court of Massachusetts. Marriage is an institution between a man and a woman. I will support an amendment to the Massachusetts Constitution to make that expressly clear."[4] Romney also maintains his opposition to same-sex civil unions that offer equivalent benefits to marriage because of the lack of distinction other than in name. In contrast, Romney's support of the institution of marriage as a union between a man and a woman has reportedly increased his status with conservatives.

In response to Obama's endorsement of same-sex marriage, Romney reiterated his opposing stance and went on to opine that the Defense of Marriage Act is "well-constructed and should be maintained." Romney further explained his views with regard to the federal government's involvement

---

3. Ashley Killough, "Obama Calls for Marriage Equality, Says 'I Want Everyone Treated Fairly,'" *CNN*, May 14, 2012, accessed August 14, 2012, http://www.cnn.com/2012/05/14/politics/obama-gay-marriage/index.html.

4. 2012 Republican Candidates: Same Sex Marriage, accessed August 14, 2012, http://2012.republican-candidates.org/Romney/Same-Sex.php.

in same-sex rights by specifying that the federal government should "allow states to determine what rights would be provided for people of the same gender that wanted to have a relationship."[5]

Discussion Questions

1. Has President Obama altered his position on gay marriage since the 2008 presidential campaign?
2. Describe the Defense of Marriage Act (DOMA) and why its constitutionality has been challenged.
3. Do you agree with President Obama's statement that, "we have never gone wrong when we've extended rights and responsibilities to everybody"? Defend your position with examples.
4. Governor Romney argues that individual states should decide on the rights and benefits of same-sex couples. What are the advantages and disadvantages of this approach?
5. In your opinion, how important is the issue of same-sex marriage to voters in this up-coming election?
6. Is marriage a civil right?

----

5. Ibid.

Healthcare Reform

Denise Yu

Republicans and Democrats agree that the U.S. healthcare system needs reform. The United States spends more on healthcare than any country in the world per capita and as a portion of total GDP (the size of the country's economy). However, Americans as a whole do not receive the best care, as shown by measures such as life expectancy (where the United States ranks 42nd). Over 15 percent of American citizens do not have health insurance; yet for those who can afford it, the most advanced treatments can be found in the United States. The debate about healthcare has focused on how to lower costs, improve care, and increase coverage, without eliminating the option to buy the best care available.

This debate has a turbulent history. A national plan to provide healthinsurance to all American citizens was first supported in a presidential campaign by Theodore Roosevelt in 1912. By the 1950s, the current model of employer-based health insurance became prominent. Since then, several major reforms have been enacted. In 1965 President Lyndon Johnson signed into law Medicare and Medicaid, programs that provide healthcare to the elderly, poor, blind, and disabled. In 1973, Richard Nixon signed the Health Maintenance Organization (HMO) law, funding the creation of group insurance plans (HMOs) meant to prevent illnesses in communities rather than treat them after the fact, when it is more expensive. In 1986, Ronald Reagan signed two new laws, one that required hospitals to treat all emergency room patients in need of immediate care even if they do not have health insurance, and another that allowed people to keep their employer's insurance for 18 months after losing their job. Each of these reforms was the result of vigorous debate, and each required at least some support from both Democrats and Republicans to pass.

When he took office in 2009, President Barack Obama called on Congress to pass comprehensive healthcare reform to solve the problems of cost, quality, and coverage. Most Republicans flat-out rejected plans to increase the role of government in healthcare provision, while more liberal Democrats wanted a single-payer system, which would allow all Americans to buy the same insurance. Mr. Obama proposed instead that the current insurance system should remain, with the addition of a government-run "public option." This proposal failed, and Obama and Congress ultimately compromised by including an "individual mandate" requiring all those who can afford to buy health insurance to do so. The intent of the mandate was to increase the pool of people in the health insurance system, thereby lowering the overall cost of insurance for everybody and reducing the number of uninsured people relying on free (and expensive) emergency room care. Proponents of the mandate argue that expanding coverage is the best way to reduce the cost because it encourages individuals to seek preventative care earlier, thus saving insurers and patients more on long-term costs. Under the mandate, there is a tax penalty for citizens who can afford insurance but do not buy it. Although no Republicans supported the final bill with the mandate in place, Congress passed the Patient Protection and

Affordable Care Act, which became law on March 23, 2010. Some of the law's provisions have already gone into effect.

Shortly after its passage, however, several individuals, states, and lobbying groups, with the support of congressional Republicans, sued the federal government over the law, saying that the individual mandate was unconstitutional because it required all citizens to purchase a good. They argued that because of the Tenth Amendment, which leaves all powers not expressly given to the federal government up to the states and the people, the federal government could not require people to buy insurance. Those believing in the constitutionality of the mandate asserted that insurance is a form of interstate commerce (commerce across state borders) and therefore the mandate to buy insurance is covered by the Commerce Clause of the Constitution, which gives the federal government the right to regulate interstate commerce. The case went to the Supreme Court, which decided on June 28, 2012, that the mandate and the law in its entirety is constitutional. Although the Court agreed that insurance did not count as interstate commerce, it ruled that the mandate was constitutional because it was a tax, similar to the federal taxes required of all citizens who can afford to pay them. Unless Congress chooses to reverse the law, the Affordable Care Act will continue to be implemented, becoming fully effective by 2020.

The election debates surrounding healthcare reform will center mainly on federal insurance mandates, reproductive care, and the future of Medicaid and Medicare. Republicans have advocated for reduced federal power in the healthcare system and have offered cost-cutting alternatives such as capping malpractice damages awards and promoting competition among insurance providers. Both sides generally agree that reform is necessary, but proposals for fixing healthcare in America are firmly divided along party lines. Even so, both sides believe that insurers should not be able to deny or cancel coverage to patients based on pre-existing conditions.

Governor Mitt Romney passed a healthcare law in Massachusetts that was similar to the Affordable Care Act when he served as governor, but he has opposed Mr. Obama's law, saying that he does not support the law's provisions on a federal level. His plan for national healthcare would be to issue an executive order that paves the way for the federal government to issue "Obamacare" waivers to all fifty states. Then he would work with Congress to repeal the full legislation and pursue policies that give each state the power to craft a healthcare reform plan that is best for its own citizens. As his website states, "the federal government's role will be to help markets work by creating a level playing field for competition."

Reproductive healthcare and access to proper healthcare for women has been connected to the health reform issue as well. The Obama administration has supported the inclusion of contraception coverage in reform bills, maintaining that access to reproductive care is a basic right of women and families as well as a necessary component for reducing overall healthcare expenditures. Governor Romney and the Republicans have pushed for reducing or eliminating federal funding for reproductive care services and organizations such as Planned Parenthood, arguing that taxpayers should not be compelled to fund services against which they have religious or ideological disagreement.

Discussion Questions

1. Make a timeline of healthcare reform over the last one hundred years.

2. Describe in your own words the "individual mandate" in President Obama's healthcare law.
3. Why did certain organizations and advocacy groups take the government to the Supreme Court over the individual mandate?
4. Outline how Governor Romney and the Republicans propose to fix the healthcare system and reduce costs.
5. Why do you think the issue of reproductive healthcare and healthcare for women is a contentious issue for many Americans?

Public Safety and Civil Liberties

Robert Hunter

Rates of violent crime in the United States have fallen dramatically over the last 20 years, a trend that public officials are eager to continue.[1] Yet once convicted felons have served their sentences, they often face discrimination in employment, housing, and other public benefits. Given these trends, this year's presidential candidates need to think not only about further crime reduction strategies but also about how to work toward a fairer justice system.

At the center of the debate over crime and criminal justice is the American prison system. The United States incarcerates a higher percentage of its population than any other country in the world.[2] This is true of juvenile detention as well, with

---

1. Daniel B. Wood, "US Crime Rate at Lowest Point in Decades. Why America Is Safer Now," *Christian Science Monitor*, January 9, 2012, accessed July 24, 2012, http://www.csmonitor.com/USA/Justice/2012/0109/US-crime-rate-at-lowest-point-in-decades.-Why-America-is-safer-now.

2. "Prison Population Rates per 100,000 of the National Population," International Centre for Prison Studies, accessed July 24, 2012, http://www.prisonstudies.org/info/worldbrief/wpb_stats.php?area=all&category=wb_poprate.

almost 100,000 young people in American jails as of 2008.[3] Proponents of tough enforcement that includes strong sentencing laws meant to prevent crime may look upon large prison populations as a necessary consequence of those policies. Those who argue for prison reform, however, believe that too much money is spent on incarceration rather than crime prevention, education, and rehabilitation, all of which they argue can save money and reduce more crime in the long run.

President Barack Obama supports drug courts and sentencing offenders to drug treatment programs rather than prisons. Governor Mitt Romney supports more punitive strategies such as "three strikes and you're out" laws, which impose mandatory sentences for people who have committed three offenses. While Mr. Obama has supported alternatives to detention strategies both in principle and as a cost-cutting technique, Mr. Romney, maintaining that those who break current laws should be punished, has proposed that states should contract with for-profit prison companies to continue expanding prison populations in order to keep up with current rates of incarceration.

Furthermore, the next president will have big decisions to make next year about how drug arrests are made and what their consequences will be. Currently, the Drug Enforcement Agency (DEA) has the power to change a drug's "schedule," or classification, which then determines what sort of punishment someone will receive for illegal possession of that drug. Marijuana and other "schedule I" drugs are the most commonly prosecuted and are considered the most dangerous by the DEA, meaning that the president can influence how they

---

3. "Prisoners in 2008," Bureau of Justice Statistics, December 2009, accessed July 24, 2012, http://bjs.ojp.usdoj.gov/content/pub/pdf/p08.pdf, 8.

are policed. In the last 15 years, police departments in dozens of big cities have taken on "stop and frisk" policies, which allow them to stop anyone if they have "reasonable suspicion" that the person is committing, has committed, or is about to commit an illegal act. Many of these arrests are for drugs like marijuana. In New York City alone, police made over 680,000 stops last year. Proponents of "stop and frisk" say the policy acts as a drug-abuse deterrent and prevents violent crime, while others claim it does not stop crime but instead excuses racial profiling and creates distrust of the police.

Neither Mr. Obama nor Mr. Romney can change how all police will act (especially because local police departments are run by city governments), but they can change the rules about how drugs are classified and thus how drug offenders are punished. Getting rid of marijuana's Schedule I classification, for instance, could eliminate thousands of low-level arrests each year. Mr. Romney has staunchly opposed calls to legalize and regulate marijuana, making a moral argument against such a change by claiming that pot legalization is simply a pet issue of a "pleasure-seeking generation that never grew up."[4] Mr. Obama and Mr. Romney have both opposed the legalization of marijuana, but Obama has claimed that he sympathizes with young users, especially because of his own youthful drug experimentation.

U.S. drug policy also affects the United States' relationship with Mexico because Mexican drug traffickers sell in high quantities to Americans. As many as 60,000 people have died in Mexico as a result of drug-related violence in the last

---

4. Mitt Romney, *No Apology: The Case for American Greatness* (New York: St. Martin's Press, 2010), 261.

six years, and Mexican officials have repeatedly called for a shift in the United States' approach to drug law enforcement.[5] Instead of employing significant resources toward low-level arrests, as the United States does now, Mexico hopes to "adjust the strategy [to] focus on certain type of crimes, like kidnapping, homicide, extortion." This will require American cooperation in the form of relaxing low-level drug arrests.[6]

Both President Obama and Governor Romney have indicated a willingness to talk to Mexican leaders about collaboration and have admitted the need to address large-scale demand for drugs in the United States, but neither candidate has issued specific policy statements on the best way to do so. Each man's future stance on this issue will be informed by his ability to work internationally on a plan that will protect public safety and keep enforcement costs down, without compromising the moral arguments that he has already laid out.

Another important issue related to public safety and civil liberties is gun control, especially in light of the number of gun-related violent crimes in America. Questions about gun control are particularly relevant in the wake of the mass murder that took place in Aurora, Colorado on July 20 during a movie premiere. America ranks among the top 15 countries

5. Doug Bandow, "Will Mexico Declare Peace in the War on Drugs, and Will Obama Let Them?" *Forbes*, July 7, 2012, accessed July 24, 2012, http://www.forbes.com/sites/dougbandow/2012/07/09/will-mexico-declare-peace-in-the-war-on-drugs-and-will-obama-let-them/.

6. Mari Hayman, "Mexico Drug War Fueled by U.S. Assault Weapons and Drug Demand, Calderón Says," Latin America News Dispatch, accessed, http://latindispatch.com/2011/09/19/mexico-drug-war-fueled-by-u-s-assault-weapons-and-drug-demand-calderon-says/.

for gun-related deaths in the world—higher than all but Estonia.[7] These statistics, coupled with a series of tragic and highly publicized shootings, have led many citizens and organizations to call for stricter control of gun sales. But the Second Amendment grants the right to bear arms, and polls consistently show that slightly more Americans favor gun rights than gun control.[8]

Both Mr. Obama and Mr. Romney have confirmed their support for the right to bear arms. During the 2008 presidential campaign, Mr. Obama supported some reform, such as reinstating the assault weapons ban and closing a loophole allowing the purchase of guns without a background check, but he has not advocated for these changes as president. Mr. Romney, as governor of Massachusetts, signed minor gun control legislation and a major assault weapons ban, but this legislation included significant pro-gun measures as well. Like Mr. Obama, he is unlikely to push for major gun reform if elected.

Discussion Questions

1. How do U.S. incarceration rates compare to other nations?
2. In what ways do President Obama and Governor Romney differ in their approach to managing the increasing prison population?

---

7. E. G. Krug, K. E. Powell, and L. L. Dahlberg, "Firearm-Related Deaths in the United States and 35 Other High- and Upper-Middle-Income Countries," *International Journal of Epidemiology* 27 (1998), 214–221, accessed July 24, 2012, http://ije.oxfordjournals.org/content/27/2/214.full.pdf.

8. Rachel Weiner, "How President Obama Changed the Gun Debate," *Washington Post*, July 23, 2012, accessed July 24, 2012, http://www.washingtonpost.com/blogs/the-fix/post/how-president-obama-changed-the-gun-debate/2012/07/23/gJQAY98u4W_blog.html.

3. Describe the power the president of the United States has to influence how drug crime is investigated and prosecuted. Is this use of executive authority justified?
4. To what extent do you agree with Governor Romney's moral argument against the legalization or regulation of marijuana? Defend your position.
5. Outline the reasons why both candidates appear keen to cooperate internationally with Mexico to prevent drug crime.
6. In light of America's high gun-related death statistics and the recent shooting in Colorado, do you think that candidates should pledge to take a tougher stance on gun control? Justify your position.

ECONOMIC POLICY

Campaign Finance Reform

Andrew Howard

The 2008 presidential election set records for campaign spending. Then-senator Barack Obama aggressively fundraised his way to new heights in campaign spending, calling upon a vast network of grassroots volunteers and donors largely through savvy use of the Internet. Mr. Obama's challenger, Senator John McCain, a co-author of the McCain-Feingold Act of 2002, the first major reform for campaign financing in 30 years, was unable to match Obama's populist momentum, and raised nearly half the money that his opponent did. However, both parties spent more on the 2008 election than in any previous election, and doubled the amount spent in the 2004 presidential race.

Candidates raise money through private donations via fundraisers and through individual contributions. These funds are sought out through direct mail or phone-based campaigns, as well as through stump speeches and other in-person appearances by the candidate. In order to maintain the transparency of these donations, the Federal Election Commission (FEC) enforces a number of regulatory limitations on campaign finance. Without these limitations, many worry that votes could be purchased by donors making significant contributions, especially wealthy contributors with private interests, non-profit organizations, private corporations, and unions. FEC regulations favor limits on individual donations and require disclosure. These measures require the names, employers, and contributions of individual donors giving over $200 to be logged into a database for public access.[1]

Political Action Committees—known as PACs—have found ways to limit the effects of FEC regulations, however. Before 2010, PACs were funded in the same limited manner as individual, private donations. However, in 2010, the conservative PAC Citizens United sued the FEC, which resulted in a Supreme Court decision that essentially gave corporations and unions the right to spend unlimited funds on political advertisements, under the justification that spending money is a form of free speech. Since individual citizens have the right to speak freely about political matters, the Court asserted, corporations are allowed to do the same. After the decision, new organizations formed, called "Super PACs," which raise and use large donations freely. The difference between donations from individuals and donations from Super PACs is the amount of money accessible to corporations, who are providing up to 23 percent of all Super PAC funds.[2]

The development of Super PACs has blurred the lines between "hard" money (documented, regulated donations) and "soft" money (anonymous, unregulated donations). While the FEC was designed to limit soft money, Super PACs can use

1. "Campaign Finance Reform: An Overview," National Conference of State Legislatures, October 3, 2011, accessed July 23, 2012, http://www.ncsl.org/legislatures-elections/elections/campaign-finance-an-overview.aspx.

2. T. W. Farnam, "Corporations Are Sending More Contributions to Super PACs," *Washington Post*, February 6, 2012, accessed July 23, 2012, http://www.washingtonpost.com/politics/corporations-are-sending-more-contributions-to-super-pacs/2012/02/02/glQAL4dYlQ_story.html.

unlimited, undocumented funds to advance a particular cause. On the surface, they are not tied to one candidate or another, yet they can produce political advertisements advancing the cause of electing (or in many cases, not electing) a specific candidate.

PACs are not regulated as strictly as individual donations. Many PACs are funded through union dues or individual employee contributions to corporately owned PACs. Additionally, PACs formed around particular candidates are often funded through individual donations that far exceed FEC regulations. For example, Restore Our Future, a Super PAC supporting Governor Mitt Romney, was created by former aides from Romney's 2008 presidential election committee. The largest single contribution was $4 million from Bob J. Perry, who funded Swift Boat Veterans for Truth, an organization that attacked Democratic candidate John Kerry's military service and character in the 2004 election. Priorities USA Action, the leading Super PAC supporting reelection for President Obama, has received sizable donations from left-leaning people in the entertainment industry, notably comedian and television show host Bill Maher, who very publicly donated one million dollars.[3]

While supporters argue that requiring Super PACs to disclose their donors may increase transparency in political contributions, it would do little to address discrepancies in donation amounts. When large corporations are funding political causes, the question is one of equality—without equal access to advertising, can there be a fair fight between the two candidates?

---

3. "Who's Financing the 'Super PACs,'" *New York Times*, May 7, 2012, accessed July 23, 2012, http://www.nytimes.com/interactive/2012/01/31/us/politics/super-pac-donors.html.

Both nominees certainly have much to gain from raising large sums of money and from ads put together and paid for by independent PACs. (These ads are the ones that attack one candidate but do not feature the spoken "I approve this message" disclaimer from the other.) Mr. Obama described the *Citizens United* decision as "a major victory for big oil, Wall Street banks, health insurance companies and the other powerful interests that marshal their power every day in Washington to drown out the voices of everyday Americans."[4] In a 2010 press statement, Mr. Romney supported the Supreme Court's decision, responding that "the first amendment right of free speech should be guaranteed not just to labor union corporations and media corporations, but equally to all corporations, big and small."[5]

Campaign finance affects how a candidate deals with and is supported by corporations. PACs and Super PACs employ highly skilled strategists, analysts, and media specialists to constantly create and distribute material, most obviously television ads, that can efficiently inform, misinform, manipulate, or confuse voters, which can leave underfunded candidates unable to respond in a timely or effective manner. While both presidential candidates have spoken about the matter in terms of the *Citizens United* decision and its unprecedented effect on fundraising, Romney is clearly ahead of Obama in terms of Super PAC spending—his Restore Our

---

4. "Statement from the President on Today's Supreme Court Decision," The White House, January 21, 2010, accessed July 23, 2012, http://www. whitehouse.gov/the-press-office/statement-president-todays-supreme-court-decision-0.

5. "Mitt Romney's Remarks to CPAC 2010," *National Review Online*, February 18, 2010, accessed July 23, 2012, http://www.nationalreview.com/corner/195046/mitt-romneys-remarks-cpac-2010/nro-staff.

Future PAC has raised more than quadruple the total collected by Priorities USA Action.[6] The 2012 election will be another record-breaking year in campaign spending, and until the Supreme Court is inclined to reverse or amend its *Citizens United* decision, the sums spent on running for office will only continue to rise.

Discussion Questions

1. What do you think President Obama meant when he stated that the Supreme Court's decision to uphold the right of corporations and unions to contribute to political campaigns is "a major victory for big oil, Wall Street banks, health insurance companies and . . . other powerful interests"?
2. What are the differences in fundraising rules between the 2008 and 2012 campaigns?
3. How does the First Amendment right of free speech relate to the financing of presidential campaigns.
4. Is it important that financial contributions—whether to Super PACs or directly to the campaigns—are transparent to the public? Why or why not?
5. Is there a danger in the current trend of greatly increased election campaign spending? Explain.

---

6. Callum Borchers, "Super PAC Backing Mitt Romney Reportedly Spending $7.2 Million on Ads During Olympics," *Boston.com*, July 5, 2012, accessed July 23, 2012, http://www.boston.com/politicalintelligence/2012/07/05/super-pac-backing-mitt-romney-reportedly-spending-million-ads-during-olympics/tTGKGz0Q5C3d420MjTRKtK/story.html.

Immigration

Ross Duncan

Since the first settlers landed in New England, the United States has been a nation of immigrants from myriad nations across the globe. By the end of the nineteenth century, however, Congress began to take measures to close America's gates. Most significantly, the Immigration Act of 1924 limited the number of immigrants to 150,000 by federal quota, and Asian immigration was prohibited entirely.[1] In the wake of the civil rights movement, the Immigration and Nationality Act of 1965 overhauled this quota system by shifting from national quotas to a preference system that favored meritocracy and family ties, while maintaining a cap on the number of visas issued annually. America became a nation of immigrants once more; in the three decades following the act, three times more immigrants were admitted to the United States than in the 30 years prior to its passage.[2]

The modern benchmark for immigration reform is the Immigration Reform and Control Act of 1986. At the time, it

---

1. "Key Dates and Landmarks in United States Immigration History," Harvard University Library Open Collections Program, accessed July 31, 2012, http://ocptest.hul.harvard.edu/timeline.html.

2. "U.S. Immigration Since 1965," History.com, accessed July 31, 2012, http://www.history.com/topics/us-immigration-since-1965.

was thought that 3 million illegal immigrants lived in the United States. This law granted a conditional pardon and protection from deportation to a majority of those immigrants. It also tightened border security and gave the federal government the ability to punish employers who knowingly employed undocumented workers. It was believed these measures would do much to stem the influx of undocumented persons into the country. In 2012, however, an estimated 10 to 12 million illegal immigrants live in the United States. It is clear that earlier attempts to end the influx of illegal immigration have failed.[3] With this in mind, both Republicans and Democrats seek reform of a battered system.

There are likely to be two key focal points of this ideological clash in this election. The first is the Support Our Law Enforcement and Safe Neighborhoods Act of 2010, an Arizona state law that was partially struck down by a 5-3 Supreme Court decision on June 25, 2012. The second is the Obama administration's proposed Development, Relief and Education for Alien Minors (DREAM) Act, which promises conditional permanent residency to younger illegal immigrants of "good moral character" who have graduated from U.S. high schools and lived in the country for at least five years prior to the bill, with additional benefits to those who complete bachelor's degrees or serve in the military.[4]

The Supreme Court overturned most of the Arizona law, determining that immigration law and enforcement are

---

3. Douglas Goodman, "Obama Immigration Reform: The Past Can Provide the Answer," Policymic, accessed July 31, 2012, http://www.policymic.com/articles/10989/obama-immigration-reform-the-past-can-provide-the-answer.

4. "Bill Summary and Status, 108th Congress (2003–2004)," Library of Congress Thomas, accessed July 31, 2012, http://thomas.loc.gov/cgi-bin/bdquery/z?d108:SN01545:@@@L&summ2=m&.

primarily the domain of the federal government and that the Arizona law went "too far" in asserting states' rights.[5] However, the decision left the most controversial part of the law intact, a provision allowing police to compel individuals to prove their residency status while enforcing other laws, as long as they have "reasonable suspicion." A large part of the controversy is the fear that this will essentially become a tool for racial profiling and discrimination against the Latino community in Arizona. Civil rights groups express further concerns that the ability of police to compel residents to "prove their innocence" with regard to their residency is a fundamental injustice, an invasion of privacy, and a disturbing and questionable assertion of state power.

Writing the dissenting opinion on the Supreme Court's decision with regard to the Arizona law, Justice Antonin Scalia summarizes the general feeling of those in favor of reform through harsher and more consistent punishment: "[Arizona's] citizens feel themselves under siege by large numbers of illegal immigrants who invade their property, strain their social services and even place their lives in jeopardy . . . and will be able to compete openly with Arizona citizens for employment." The concern is that laxness in federal enforcement allows illegal immigrants, simply by virtue of being in the country, to leech resources from legitimate citizens and permanent residents. Partially this is a classic argument over scarce resources. Each state only has so much money, land, and jobs to provide—even to its fully legitimate citizens. Added to this is moral outrage that stems from a belief that these

---

5. Fawn Johnson, "The Supreme Court Decides (Mostly) Against Arizona in Immigration Case," *The Atlantic*, June 25, 2012, accessed July 31, 2012, http://www.theatlantic.com/national/archive/2012/06/the-supreme-court-decides-mostly-against-arizona-in-immigration-case/258925/.

illegal immigrants cause this drain knowingly and to benefit themselves, while flouting the laws of the country that supports them. Amnesty and lax enforcement then only encourage more illegal immigration and more of the aforementioned problems, and it indirectly punishes the law-abiding taxpayer for the illegal activity of others. Those who support stronger immigration control also often do so to prevent crime. Living under the radar, as illegal immigrants must do, to some degree necessitates participation in less than legitimate activities, whether that is working below minimum wage or involvement with gangs and organized crime. Such are the arguments made by those that push for tighter restrictions and more consistent, harsher punishments.

It is a matter of opinion whether federal policy is indeed lax. The Supreme Court cited the number of annual deportations at nearly 400,000—a number expected to grow. The system may be ineffectual because it is overburdened, not because it is excessively forgiving.[6] President Barack Obama has stated his opposition to the Arizona law, viewing it as an assault on fairness. Governor Mitt Romney on the other hand supports several sections of the law, while principally defending the right of states to write their own immigration-related legislation.[7]

The DREAM Act reflects an opposing view of how best to deal with the issue of illegal immigration. This solution would selectively absorb potentially productive alien residents

6. Robert M. Morgenthau, "Supreme Court Immigration Ruling in Arizona v. U.S. Got It Backward," *Daily Beast*, July 11, 2012, accessed July 31, 2012, http://www.thedailybeast.com/articles/2012/07/11/supreme-court-immigration-ruling-in-arizona-v-u-s-got-it-backward.html.

7. Liz Halloran, "Where They Stand: Obama, Romney on Immigration," NPR, July 11, 2012, accessed July 31, 2012, http://www.npr.org/2012/07/06/156381703/where-they-stand-obama-romney-on-immigration.

(immigrants) into the American citizenry in order to reduce many of the problems related to crime and resource drain. Arguably, by providing opportunities for these younger immigrants to become properly educated, fully contributing citizens, the United States would benefit more from their continued presence and productivity than through their deportation. The DREAM Act also appeals to the moral intuition that the children of illegal immigrants ought not to be punished for the transgressions of their parents, which is likely the reason the act specifically targets "alien minors."

This act would do little to assuage the fears of those who support stricter enforcement on the grounds that illegal immigrants potentially take the jobs of legitimate citizens. However, it would at least ensure that those granted amnesty under DREAM would be working "above board," and would be unlikely to participate in criminal activity or to undercut unskilled legal labor by working for less than minimum wage. Critics argue that by continuing to grant amnesty, the act rewards and encourages illegal immigrants. They also fear fraud by illegal immigrants who would not be covered under the act—most notably gang members exempted by the "good moral standing" clause.

Mitt Romney has stated that while he personally opposes the bill, he does support the idea of granting permanent citizenship to illegal immigrants who honorably serve in the U.S. military. President Obama supports the idea of allowing foreign college students to remain in the United States after graduation.[8] On June 15, 2012, Mr. Obama controversially used executive authority to stop the deportation of illegal immigrants who may qualify under the DREAM Act. This is

----

8. Halloran.

not a permanent shift in law but, according to the President, a "temporary stopgap measure." Republicans were angry at what they saw as an overreach of authority, claiming that Obama had done an unfairly gone ahead without approval from Congress.[9]

One of the few policies that both party leaders agree on is the construction of a fence along the border with Mexico, though Republicans tend to believe Mr. Obama did not go far enough in ensuring security when construction of the initial fence was completed in 2011. Both Mr. Obama and Mr. Romney supported the failed 2007 Immigration Reform bill that attempted to find a pathway to citizenship for some illegal immigrants. Mr. Romney has since denounced the attempted legislation as an "amnesty plan."[10] However, one could generally say that Republicans support the rule of law over social tinkering, and consequently support stricter and harsher immigration laws.

Conversely, Democrats are typically in favor of modifying existing legislation to create what they view as a more beneficial social environment. Their policies tend to be more a reflection of where they want society to go in the future, rather than a strict upholding of the law as it exists now. Although these are generalizations of the views held by both parties, they do help illuminate the issue of immigration reform within a greater sociopolitical context.

---

9. Julia Preston and John H. Cushman Jr., "Obama to Permit Young Migrants to Remain in U.S.," *New York Times*, June 15, 2012, accessed July 31, 2012, http://www.nytimes.com/2012/06/16/us/us-to-stop-deporting-some-illegal-immigrants.html.

10. Halloran.

Discussion Questions

1. According to the essay, how many illegal immigrants are estimated to live in the United States today?
2. How might Arizona's Support Our Law Enforcement and Safe Neighborhoods Act of 2010 affect the Latino community in that state?
3. Is federal immigration policy lax? Explain your perspective.
4. Do you agree that Obama's DREAM Act "rewards and encourages" illegal immigrants?
5. Republican leaders believed President Obama's use of executive authority in June 2012 to prevent the deportation of some illegal immigrants to be an "overreach of authority." Do you agree with them? Why or why not?
6. What are the moral arguments for and against allowing foreign college students to remain within the United States after graduation, which President Obama has proposed?

National Debt

Roger Sollenberger

The debate over the national debt is one of the biggest, yet least understood, issues of the 2012 election cycle. The mechanisms behind the debt are numerous and complex, and economists do not agree on the terms of the total. The media suggests estimates from $11 trillion to $16 trillion. According to the Treasury Department, the national debt is $15.9 trillion.[1] The size of the debt is important because limitless spending is unsustainable, and if the United States ever defaults on payment, it would not only wreck the U.S. economy but would also send the global economy into depression.

It is important to note that the debt has not *caused* anything; instead, it is a consequence of choices the country has made in taxing and spending. Every year the government must raise money to run its programs, pay its employees, and provide the services we enjoy as a nation—services including things like the military, Social Security, Medicare/Medicaid, highways and infrastructure, scientific research, and education. These services are popular, and many are essential, but they are

---

1. Combined total debt held by the public—the sum of public debt and intra-governmental holdings—according to U.S. Treasury as of July 11, 2012. "The Debt to the Penny and Who Holds It," TreasuryDirect, accessed July 24, 2012, http://www.treasurydirect.gov/NP/BPDLogin?application=np.

costly, so to fund them we need an enormous annual federal budget.[2] The government can finance its budget a few ways: raising taxes, which is politically unpopular; printing money, which leads to inflation; or borrowing money, which creates the debt, through the sale of U.S. Treasury bonds. Borrowing is convenient because it allows the government to spend more money than it makes: it means services aren't limited to what the government can pay for today. Instead, when the United States borrows, it has access to all the financial resources that any entity[3] would want to lend on credit; the United States will pay them back with interest at some future date. Borrowing pays for expensive government services and allows Americans and American businesses to hang onto their money and spend it in the economy, which in general spurs growth. However, when the government borrows and spends more than it takes in, it runs a deficit. The national debt is the unpaid total of budget deficits, plus interest, year after year.[4]

In recent years, the debt has skyrocketed. In 2001, the debt was around $6 trillion, and the White House reports an increase of $12.7 trillion in the last decade.[5] This is an unsustainable trajectory, and according to the Congressional

---

2. The federal budget has been increasing every year. President Obama's proposed budget for 2013 is $3.8 trillion, but has little chance of passing the Republican House. Read the entire budget proposal at: http://www.washingtonpost.com/blogs/ezra-klein/post/federal-budget-read-the-full-document/2012/02/13/gIQA3Wy1AR_blog.html, accessed August 1, 2012.

3. The United States actually owes the biggest single chunk of its debt to itself, though it also is indebted to other countries. To see a chart of countries and other entities that hold U.S. debt, see "Who Really Owns the U.S. National Debt," MyGovCost.org, accessed July 24, 2012, http://www.mygovcost.org/2012/04/02/who-really-owns-the-us-national-debt/.

4. The only year the U.S. government paid off its debts was 1835.

5. "U.S. National Debt," The White House, accessed July 24, 2012, http://www.whitehouse.gov/infographics/us-national-debt.

Budget Office,[6] the interest payments alone[7] could bankrupt the government in the not-too-distant future. The danger is that if the people, businesses, and other countries who have lent money to the government begin to doubt that it can pay back what it has borrowed, they will stop lending money, which means it will be harder for the government to come up with money to fund services, and much harder to pay off the enormous debt already owed. Some of these creditors may even request that the government pay them back immediately, and if everybody does this at once, the U.S. Treasury will not be able to pay back all of those loans and will go bankrupt. The War on Terror, steadily increasing healthcare costs, the tax cuts passed by President George W. Bush in 2001 and 2003, tax revenue lost to the recession, and economic stimulus[8] have all contributed to the national debt.

The national debt forms the intersection for two huge 2012 campaign issues: the state of the economy, and the role of government in Americans' lives. The debt is tied inextricably to government spending, taxes, the stimulus bills, national defense, and entitlement programs like Social Security. Because many American families are currently facing tough economic choices themselves, the debt debate has also been infused with strong emotions and values: themes of outrage, justice, and responsibility. One popular analogy for

---

6. "Report: CBO's Long-Term Budget Outlook," The Committee for a Responsible Federal Budget," accessed July 24, 2012, http://crfb.org/document/report-cbo's-long-term-budget-outlook.

7. In 2011, debt interest payments alone were over $454 billion. See "Interest Expense on the Debt Outstanding," TreasuryDirect, accessed July 24, 2012, http://www.treasurydirect.gov/govt/reports/ir/ir_expense.htm.

8. White House numbers on debt and recession revenue also here: "U.S. National Debt," The White House, accessed July 24, 2012, http://www.whitehouse.gov/infographics/us-national-debt.

the national debt that plays on these emotions — one you're likely to hear both candidates use — is that the government is basically a family running up a credit card. This is a misleading comparison, however, because the government's debt is much more complex than a family budget.

Governor Romney's budget proposal promises to cut spending. He proposes to balance the budget by repealing the Patient Protection and Affordable Care Act (also known as "Obamacare") and eliminating all "nonessential" government spending, while extending the full Bush tax cuts and leaving the defense budget untouched. He will point to President Obama's policies — the stimulus, the Affordable Care Act — and to the debt that has increased by $5 trillion on Obama's watch, and claim the Obama administration hasn't been a responsible custodian of the economy.[9] Mr. Romney himself has not been specific about what he considers nonessential spending, but as a candidate he may not have to be. He wants to make the case that he is the candidate who will make the necessary tough decisions to whip the country back into shape. His is a populist argument: taxpayers ought to use their money how they see fit, and the country must bring an irresponsible government under control or face financial catastrophe.

President Obama proposed a budget[10] that significantly increases taxes on the wealthiest Americans[11] and biggest

---

9. Read up on Romney's position here: "Fiscal Responsibility," Mitt Romney for President, accessed July 24, 2012, http://www.mittromney.com/issues/fiscal-responsibility.

10. Read the entire budget proposal at: http://www.washingtonpost.com/blogs/ezra-klein/post/federal-budget-read-the-full-document/2012/02/13/gIQA3Wy1AR_blog.html, accessed July 25, 2012.

11. Ezra Klein, "Comparing Taxes Under Obama's and Romney's Budgets," accessed July 24, 2012, http://www.washingtonpost.com/blogs/ezra-klein/post/comparing-obamas-and-romneys-budgets/2011/08/25/gIQA0q35AR_blog.html?hpid=z1.

American businesses. He will acknowledge the debt must be controlled, and point to what he believes are the successes of his spending, such as the economic recovery, and all the money that the Affordable Care Act will actually save the country. The president also proposes significant cuts to "excessive" defense spending, and will say he ended a costly and unnecessary war in Iraq and is bringing the troops home from a protracted engagement in Afghanistan. He will agree that the country must cut spending, but with a fragile economy these cuts need to be strategic and balanced with increased revenue. In further contrast to Mr. Romney, Mr. Obama proposes to end the Bush tax cuts on those making more than $250,000, another populist argument: the little guy vs. the selfish and irresponsible business culture that caused the economic crash of 2008. And unlike Mr. Romney, Mr. Obama is obligated to govern: his argument is policy, so he must be specific and bipartisan, and his numbers must add up.

Discussion Questions

1. How does the issue of the national debt relate to the two biggest campaign issues of 2012: the state of the economy and the role of government in the economy?
2. Why do you think the national debt is such an emotionally charged issue for Americans?
3. What is Governor Romney's position on how best to deal with the national debt?
4. According to the author of the article, what does President Obama believe are the two main successes of the federal spending he has authorized?

5. Both Governor Romney and President Obama advance "populist arguments" on the national debt. What are they? Which do you find more compelling?
6. What do you think is the best way to control the national debt—reigning in government spending, as Governor Romney suggests, or ending tax cuts for the wealthy, as President Obama proposes?

Taxes

Dean DeChiaro

Since the presidency of Ronald Reagan, the federal budget and the taxes that fund it have been the most consistently debated topic in politics. This is because it is an issue from which the most difficult of questions arise: should America be run by "big government," emulating the European social welfare state, or should it mandate minimal tax regulations, leaving each citizen entirely responsible for his or her well-being? Democrats tend to advocate the former, taxing citizens according to income and providing welfare programs for the less wealthy, while Republicans are proponents of the small, decentralized state and minimal taxation. Nevertheless, how the government spends its money affects all Americans, especially in times of economic downturn.

As it currently stands, the federal budget has reached previously unsurpassed levels, estimated at about $3.7 trillion for 2012, as estimated by the Congressional Budget Office.[1] The majority of the budget goes toward the Department of Defense ($1.45 trillion), the Department of Health and Human Services ($1.11 trillion, or roughly $9,700 per household), which administers programs such as Medicare and Medicaid, and

---

1. U.S. Debt Clock, accessed August 14, 2012, http://www.usdebtclock.org.

the Social Security Administration ($808 billion).[2] Tax cuts, which some economists have argued should be counted into the budget, have most recently been estimated at $1 trillion in 2010, according to the liberal Center for American Progress.[3] The most notable tax cuts, those passed by President George W. Bush in 2001 and 2003, are set to expire on New Year's Eve this year, and are currently the most discussed topic related to taxes and spending among journalists and pundits, who have hyperbolically dubbed the sunsetting of these tax cuts "Taxmageddon."

As the 2012 presidential election approaches, each candidate's focus has been primarily on decreasing the federal debt, estimated at about $15 trillion. At its most basic level, President Barack Obama's plan draws on Keynesian economic theory, the belief that a mixed economy of public and private enterprise, bolstered by a strong welfare state, can jumpstart the economy. Governor Mitt Romney, meanwhile, advocates a Reagan-esque devotion to laissez-faire economics, arguing that with substantial tax cuts and limited regulation on private businesses, the economy will naturally grow. Specifically, Mr. Obama's plan, detailed on his website, targets tax loopholes for households with annual incomes over $250,000, via efforts such as the Buffet Rule (a stipulation in President Obama's plan which would apply a minimum tax rate of 30 percent to individuals making over $1 million per year), while simultaneously reducing taxes for middle-class families and

---

2. U.S. Federal Budget, accessed August 14, 2012, http://www.usfederalbudget. us/federal_budget_detail_fy13.

3. Seth Hanlon and Michael Linden, "Good News on Deficit Reduction: Conservatives Now Recognize Some Tax Breaks as Wasteful Spending," *Center for American Progress*, June 23, 2011, accessed August 14, 2012, http://www. americanprogress.org/issues/2011/06/conservatives_tax_breaks.html/.

small business owners. Mr. Romney, on the other hand, states on his website that he would reduce government spending from its current level, around $33,000 per household, to around $25,000, while maintaining individual tax rates but decreasing rates for private corporations.

Regarding government programs, President Obama and Governor Romney stand opposed, with Romney vowing to repeal Mr. Obama's healthcare act, saving the country around $95 billion, according to his website. He also has advocated cutting spending on social programs by 5 percent (without touching national security spending) and pulling funding from the National Endowment of the Arts and Humanities, the Corporation for Public Broadcasting, and the Legal Services Corporation. Furthermore, he plans to save up to $100 million by reducing foreign aid. Meanwhile, in September, President Obama revealed a plan to reduce the deficit by about $3.2 trillion in the next ten years via increased taxes on the American upper class and drastic reductions in defense spending.

The candidates' positions on taxes and government spending, as noted earlier, drive right to the crux of their political ideologies, and relate to their positions on other political issues. For instance, President Obama's insistence on reducing defense spending is tied closely to his desire to end America's military activities in Iraq and Afghanistan, while Romney's plan to eliminate Title X Family Planning funding draws quite publicly from his opposition to abortion rights. And while the main concern for both candidates is lowering the national deficit, the ways they would go about it are very different, and realistically would benefit very different types of Americans.

Discussion Questions

1. Identify the major expenses in the federal budget. Where do you think the next president of the United States should cut spending? Defend your position.
2. Assess the merits of President Obama's approach to reducing the deficit by increasing taxes on the wealthiest households and slashing military spending.
3. Is it justifiable that wealthier Americans are taxed more to pay for services that primarily benefit poorer Americans?
4. What do you think of Governor Romney's plans to cut spending, including saving up to $110 million by reducing foreign aid to developing nations?
5. How do the candidates' policies on taxes reflect their broader political positions?

Unemployment

A.J. Carver

Jobs are always being created and destroyed. Entrepreneurs start new businesses and hire workers and existing companies may grow and hire more people, shrink and fire people, or even go out of business. When we read headlines like "June Jobs Report: U.S. Adds 80,000 Jobs" it means that in June the total number of jobs created was 80,000 more than the total number of jobs lost. From 1980 to 1990, an average of 151,000 jobs per month were created in the United States as the population and economy grew. Between 1990 and 2001 the average increased to 178,000 jobs created per month. From 2001 to 2007 the average decreased to 68,000 jobs created per month. Then in December 2007, the "Great Recession," a slowdown in economic activity not seen since the Great Depression, began. In 2008 and 2009 an average of 361,000 jobs were lost per month.

Another useful measure of the job market is the unemployment rate. This is calculated by counting the number of people who do not have a job but have looked for one in the last four weeks, then dividing that number plus the number of people with jobs (this sum is called the labor force). The labor force is not the same as the population. Since the 1980s the labor force has been about two-thirds of the population (about

64 percent in 1980, topping 67 percent in the late 1990s, and now back to about 64 percent). Unemployment tends to go up during recessions and down in expansions. Since the 1980s, across all groups, the unemployment number has ranged from about 4 percent to 10 percent. The 10 percent recorded in October 2009 was the highest number since the early 1980s. For African-Americans the unemployment high was 16.7 percent in March 2010 and August 2011, and for Hispanics it was 13.1 percent in both August 2009 and November 2010.

Employment is integral to everything from meeting the basic survival needs of a family (affording food and shelter) all the way to achieving the heights of self-expression, such as by feeling that one is contributing to society. For this reason, politicians are often judged by the quantity and quality jobs in the economy. Both campaigns tie an improved economy to more jobs and hence lower unemployment. The debate about the economy and which candidate has better economic policies depends on such questions as "Is the economy improving or getting worse?" and "What caused the economic collapse?" President Barack Obama cites 28 consecutive months of job growth totaling 4.4 million private-sector jobs as evidence that the economy is improving. Governor Mitt Romney cites 31 consecutive months of unemployment over 8 percent and an increase in long-term unemployment as a failure of the policies of President Obama.

Mr. Romney organizes his plan for jobs and the economy into seven categories: tax, regulation, trade, energy, labor, human capital, and spending. He argues that lower taxes will stimulate entrepreneurship, job creation, and investment. He also argues regulations are like a tax because there are costs for businesses to comply. Regulations also harm businesses by scaring them away from making investments or hiring workers. On the topic of trade, Mr. Romney, like Mr. Obama, thinks more is better, under the right conditions, and believes that Obama has not done enough to foster it. He believes increasing the size of the carbon-based energy economy in the United States can create jobs and that workers need retraining but that retraining should be done by collaborations between the government and private companies, not by the government. He also believes more highly skilled immigrants who have the potential to create businesses, and therefore employ people, should be admitted to the country. He wants a government that spends less, arguing that the current national debt has created uncertainty that prevents or delays investments that could create businesses and therefore jobs.

As an incumbent, Mr. Obama has made decisions and implemented policies that can be evaluated. He argues that the economy continues to struggle because the 2008 financial crisis and the recession that followed were worse than anyone initially thought. By signing the American Recovery and Reinvestment Act (ARRA, commonly known as the Stimulus Act) in 2009, he authorized $831 billion of spending on tax benefits, infrastructure investments, and entitlement programs (such as Medicare, which provides healthcare to the elderly). He argues that this spending—over $750 billion of which has been paid out so far—was necessary and helped prevent the Great Recession from becoming the Second Great Depression.

Like Mr. Romney, Mr. Obama believes low rates of taxation can stimulate the economy—the ARRA reduced taxes for small businesses and 95 percent of individuals. In 2001 and 2003 taxes were lowered in what has become known as the Bush tax cuts, which were to expire at the end of 2010. In December

2010 President Obama signed an act that extended these tax cuts and authorized money to be spent on unemployment insurance. President Obama has signed trade deals with South Korea, Columbia, and Panama, deals that will support an estimated 70,000 jobs. He used the power of the federal government to extend emergency loans to the auto industry, an action that saved the three major auto companies from bankruptcy. Mr. Obama believes a lack of regulation and weak enforcement led to the current financial crisis. As part of the Obama-supported Dodd–Frank Wall Street Reform and Consumer Protection Act, Congress formed the newly created Consumer Financial Protection Bureau. This bureau aims to prevent practices like mortgage lenders making home loans to people who they know either don't understand or can't afford the mortgage. This matters to the economy because these loans are grouped together and sold as safe investments (the idea being that even if a few people don't pay, lenders will still get money from those that do). In 2008, when many home owners stopped paying their mortgages, the owners and the lenders couldn't tell how much the homes were worth, so lenders stopped lending and both owners and lenders stopped spending, thus precipitating the recession and destroying jobs.

Discussion Questions
1. How is the unemployment rate measured?
2. How does unemployment affect families and individuals?
3. What can be done to lower the unemployment rate?
4. How does Governor Romney's plan to fix unemployment differ from President Obama's?
5. What effect does high unemployment have on 15- to 24-year-olds?

Unions and Public Employees

Nathan Rifkin

When Wisconsin governor Scott Walker, a Republican, signed the Wisconsin budget repair bill in 2011, reducing the benefits and power of public sector unions, he propelled unions into the national spotlight and set the stage for a national conversation about the rights of public sector unions during the 2012 presidential race. Governor Walker's actions sparked massive protests, and the millions of dollars spent in Wisconsin on both sides of the issue show the enduring significance of the debate over unions.

Unions are formed when workers with a common interest come together to appoint someone to bargain on their behalf for better working conditions, wages, or benefits. Typically, unions are created on the basis of a common geographical region (for instance, all of the employees of a hotel might decide to unionize to bargain with the owners of the building), or along a common occupation (such as the nationwide American Postal Workers Union). Frequently, workers will combine these two interests and join, to use the above example, the local chapter of the American Postal Workers

Union in order to more specifically represent their interests as a postal worker in their region.

Most larger unions maintain an affiliation with one of two larger umbrella organizations.[1] The AFL-CIO (American Federation of Labor & Congress of Industrial Organizations) and the Change to Win Federation — each of which represents a wide range of unions — lobby the federal government on behalf of their member unions, trying to get legislation passed that is favorable to the interests of workers. In the same way that citizens, working within civic organizations and businesses, can ask their local government to advocate on their behalf to the state government, individual union members, through their affiliation with increasingly large and, therefore, influential unions, can attempt to influence government policy.

A further distinction remains, though, and that is the one between public sector and private sector unions. Scott Walker's bill reduced the power of unions representing public sector workers, who are employed and paid by the government. This includes teachers employed by public schools, firefighters, and the municipal employees who staff and run government agencies. Scott Walker's bill did not, however, deal with private sector unions, which represent the interests of employees working for a private company. Public sector unions are more controversial than their private sector counterparts

---

1. Measuring union membership claims is difficult due to conflicting reports and little national oversight, resulting in many union workers not being counted as such and many union workers counted multiple times due to belonging to more than one union. The AFL-CIO claims to represent 12 million workers: "AFL-CIO Unions," AFL-CIO, accessed July 10, 2012. http://www. aflcio.org/About/AFL-CIO-Unions.

The Change to Win Federation claims to represent 6 million workers: "Change to Win Coalition," *New York Times*, accessed July 10, 2012, http:// topics.nytimes.com/top/reference/timestopics/organizations/c/change_to_ win_coalition/index.html.

because they benefit from tax dollars, and more government employees—or better government employee salaries and benefits—means higher taxes and a larger government. Governor Mitt Romney and other Republicans, who typically want the size of the government reduced, come down harder against public sector unions since they represent an increase in the size of government as well as the number of tasks government performs. Currently, there are 7.6 million public sector employees in unions, representing 37 percent of all such public sector workers, compared to 7.2 million private sector workers in unions, who make up 6.9 percent of private sector workers. Both numbers represent significant declines in union membership over the past 20 years.[2]

Governor Romney and President Barack Obama disagree about unions' key purpose: increasing employee wages. Mr. Obama and the Democrats argue that without unions, workers would be paid far too little, because corporations and governments have the power to dictate terms to employees. According to Democrats, only unions, which give workers the ability to bargain collectively with their employer, are able to secure fair wages and benefits for workers. Democrats point toward three developments as evidence that unions must be empowered to protect workers:[3] increasing corporate profits, which make up the highest percentage of the nation's GDP (the total size of its economy) since 1950; stagnant wages,

---

2. "Union Members Summary," Bureau of Labor Statistics, United States Department of Labor, January 27, 2012, accessed July 5, 2012, http://www.bls.gov/news.release/union2.nr0.htm. Numbers are likely over-reported due to redundancies in counting.

3. Rex Nutting, "Corporate Profits' Share of Pie Most in 60 Years," Marketwatch, *Wall Street Journal*, July 29, 2011, accessed July 7, 2012, http://articles.marketwatch.com/2011-07-29/commentary/30699039_1_profits-gdp-wages-and-salaries.

currently at their lowest percentage of GDP since 1955; and perpetually lower union participation rates. Democrats also argue that when the middle class and the poor earn more, they spend more, helping the economy as a whole.

Mr. Romney and the Republicans argue that the wages and benefits unions receive are too high, harming the economy and reducing the number of jobs that companies can create. Republicans point toward examples of union benefits crippling companies, such as the $134 billion pension obligation GM owed to retired United Auto Workers union members. Without government assistance, GM would have been unable to pay off the obligation and might not have survived. Republicans argue that unions artificially drive up the market price of labor, crippling businesses, raising unemployment, and reducing the total welfare of the economy.

The debate about the economic benefits of unions is likely politically motivated as well. Unions are among the top Democratic donors and volunteer organizations, and union members tend to vote Democrat by a wide margin.[4] Strong unions, therefore, benefit Democrats, since the more union members there are, the more likely Democratic voters there will be. Democrats also face union pressure, since Democrats who consistently favor pro-union policies will garner more support from unions. Conversely, Republicans benefit politically by keeping unions weak, because weaker unions are less able to help Democratic campaigns. This political dimension clouds the debate about unions, as policies that affect unions have

---

4. Callum Borchers, "Barack Obama Leads Mitt Romney Among Union Members, Poll Shows." Boston.com. June 11, 2012, accessed July 8, 2012, http://www.boston.com/politicalintelligence/2012/06/11/barack-obama-leads-mitt-romney-among-union-members-poll-shows/gUiVuq6yALnXKXp071KcrO/story.html.

clear political winners and losers. Ultimately, unions will play a role in re-electing Mr. Obama or electing Mr. Romney and will continue to play a major role in both our economy and our political culture for years to come.

Discussion Questions

1. Explain why President Obama argues that workers need unions in order to ensure they receive fair wages and benefits.
2. Why are public sector unions more "controversial" than private sector unions?
3. Compare the Democrats' economic argument that unions help the economy with Governor Romney's assertion that the opposite is true. Defend one of these positions.
4. What political reason do Republicans have for keeping unions weak?
5. Why did Governor Walker's Wisconsin budget repair bill spark massive protests, and what relevance does the bill have for the 2012 presidential elections?

FOREIGN POLICY

Afghanistan

Shawn Patterson

In few areas does the president have more discretion or power than in his duties as commander-in-chief. In this election, voters will have to decide between the views of President Barack Obama and Governor Mitt Romney on American foreign policy, and particularly on the United States' future involvement in Afghanistan. With the economy still in a recession, this issue has lost importance in recent years, but only by fully understanding the candidates' positions can voters make an informed decision that will influence America's role on the world stage.

Following the September 11 terrorist attacks, then-President George W. Bush authorized the U.S. military to invade Afghanistan with the goal of eliminating Al Qaeda, the terrorist organization responsible for 9/11, and removing the Taliban regime from power. In 2003, the United States also invaded Iraq with the goal of removing Iraqi president Saddam Hussein from power under the assumption that Hussein was supporting terrorism and developing weapons of mass destruction. This second military operation took the focus off of Afghanistan, and in the lead-up to the 2006 congressional elections Democratic candidates successfully used the increasingly unpopular foreign wars to propel the party back into control of Congress. In 2008 Democrats built on their momentum from 2006 and assembled larger majorities in Congress, while President Barack Obama won the White House.

During the Obama administration, the War in Afghanistan came back to the forefront of foreign policy. President Obama argued that the War in Iraq was waged on false pretenses and that decreasing the risk of terrorism through the conflict in Afghanistan required the full attention of the military. Throughout 2010, Mr. Obama authorized an increase of 30,000 troops in Afghanistan to assist with combat missions, known in the media as "the surge." In part because of the success of this increase, and in part because of swelling public sentiment against the war, beginning in 2011 the surge troops were slowly removed from Afghanistan. Not long after the beginning of this drawdown, Mr. Obama announced a planned end to combat missions in Afghanistan at the end of 2014.

The 2012 campaign will inevitably focus on the struggling economy, but considering the influence the president has over foreign policy, it is important for voters to consider the candidates' different visions for Afghanistan. The war has already cost the lives of at least 15,000 troops, almost 2,000 of them American,[1] and approximately 15,000 Afghan civilians,[2] as well as uncounted enemy combatants. Financially, the war has cost the United States over $500

---

1. "Operation Enduring Freedom," iCasualties, accessed July 10, 2012, http://icasualties.org/OEF/index.aspx.

2. "Afghan Civilian Deaths Rise, Insurgents Responsible for Most Casualties—UN," UN News Centre, July 14, 2011, accessed July 10, 2012, http://www.un.org/apps/news/story.asp?NewsID=39036&Cr=Afghan&Cr1.

billion.[3] But supporters of the war argue that these costs are necessary to establish democracy and security in Afghanistan, as well as to keep the United States safe from future terrorist attacks. Mr. Obama and Mr. Romney weigh these problems differently, and depending on which candidate is successful in November, the American people could witness two very different paths.

Mr. Obama's policy in Afghanistan is a combination of the campaign rhetoric that brought Democrats back into power in 2006 and his own larger vision of America's role abroad. While many argued for an immediate exit from the country, the current administration believes that only by providing a clear timetable for withdrawal can the U.S. maintain domestic support for the mission and apply the appropriate pressure on the Afghan government to provide for their own security. According to his campaign website, Mr. Obama believes that only by forcing Afghanistan to "take ownership of the security and leadership of their country," will long-term stability in the region be possible, but that goal would be impossible without short-term military assistance. This long-term strategy is also a function of the growing costs of the conflict, with a financial burden of $6.7 billion a month, and casualties exceeding 2,000 U.S. soldiers since the 2001 invasion. In that vein, the president has continued to support slowly drawing down troop levels beginning in 2012, ending combat missions and transferring authority to the Afghan Security Forces by 2014.

Governor Romney, in contrast, believes that the removal of troops after the 2010 surge was premature. General David Petraeus, who led the Afghanistan mission during the

---

3. Cost of War, accessed July 10, 2012, http://costofwar.com.

surge and now serves as director of the Central Intelligence Agency, agrees with this criticism. Mr. Romney argues that by supporting a timetable for withdrawal, the United States will only encourage "the Taliban to believe that they could wait us out," as stated on his campaign website. According to Mr. Romney, Mr. Obama's plan lacks military rationale and comes across as an overly political, election-year ploy. By contrast, Mr. Romney asserts that he would use the advice of his generals and the reports on ground conditions to determine when troop withdrawal would be appropriate. This policy acknowledges the costs of the war, but places greater importance on national security and the democratic stability of Afghanistan.

Mr. Romney believes that the United States has both a right and an obligation to stabilize foreign regimes that may pose a risk to the United States. In other words, because the United States helped establish this new government, the country has a responsibility to help rebuild Afghanistan. Considering the staggering costs and growing public discontent with the wars, Romney will have to offer a solid defense of these positions during the debates.

Discussion Questions

1. Outline the events that led then-President George W. Bush to authorize the invasion of Afghanistan in 2001.
2. In the midst of a domestic economic recession, how much weight should voters put on the candidates' foreign policy stances, such as the military operations in Afghanistan?
3. To what extent do you believe President Obama's announcement to withdraw troops from Afghanistan by the end of 2014 is an "election-year ploy"?

4. Does the United States have an obligation to ensure a stable transition to democracy in Afghanistan?
5. Can military intervention ever be justified on humanitarian grounds—such as the human rights abuses taking place in Syria—when there is no security threat to the United States?

China

Ted Mateoc

Since Richard Nixon "opened" China in 1972, China's successful economic rise has placed it at the center of foreign policy discussions in the United States. Through its diverse global economy, China vies for clout in world institutions such as the International Monetary Fund and the World Bank, and geostrategic influence in Asia, Africa, and South America. Understandably, this progression toward a world in which China could become the dominant superpower concerns many Americans.

Because China serves as a convenient boogeyman, presidential candidates have a decades-old tradition of attacking sitting presidents for their policy toward China.[1] In the campaign of 1992, Bill Clinton attacked President George H. W. Bush for "coddling dictators" only to be similarly condemned during the 2000 campaign by George W. Bush. During the 2008 presidential campaign, then-senator Barack Obama accused George W. Bush of being "patsy" to China's economic and political desires.[2] But in spite of all the scolding

---

1. Lexington, "The China-Bashing Syndrome," *The Economist*, July 14, 2012, accessed July 31, 2012, http://www.economist.com/node/21558581.

2. Ibid.

during the election, presidential candidates tend to change their positions once they reach the White House. Politicians' threats over China have yet to make the Chinese government nervous about the U.S. government's intentions, but China is in the middle of its own leadership transition, so this could change. Either way, domestic pressures encourage candidates to talk tough on China no matter how dependent the United States may be on China's continued economic prosperity. To the credit of China's government, they have seemed to recognize that the candidates' bravado is due mostly to election-time pressure.

In the first half of his term President Obama was criticized for being too soft on China, and critics argued that his policies helped fuel China's geopolitical expansion in Southeast Asia as the country increased its military spending and adopted a more confrontational approach toward territorial disputes with neighbors. Mr. Obama had campaigned against China's policy of keeping its currency artificially low in order to encourage exports and discourage imports. As president, however, he has opted for softer public and private pressure to let China's currency appreciate.

On a geopolitical level, Mr. Obama engaged in a widely publicized "pivot" strategy toward Asia, intended to reassure America's Southeast Asian allies that they can count on the United States' support against China. From the American perspective, countries would join together to contain China with the United States as the keystone but without the United States having to commit significant resources to the region. The policy has multiple components ranging from shifting military assets to Eastern and Southeastern Asia, including plans to station up to 60 percent of all naval forces in the

Pacific, an increase of 10 percent.[3] On the diplomatic side, America has joined the East Asia Summit, interceded on the South China Sea, opened a connection to Myanmar, and worked on improving relations between the United States, Australia, and India. Economically, the United States has ratified a free trade agreement with South Korea and signed the framework agreement for the Trans-Pacific Partnership. The pivot seems to have slowed China's expansion of power in the region and has been cautiously welcomed by foreign-policy analysts.[4]

Much as Mr. Obama did four years ago, Governor Mitt Romney has pledged to instruct the Treasury to treat China as a currency manipulator if given the chance, in addition to slapping intellectual property sanctions on China until the Chinese government responds to business concerns about the safety of intellectual property designs of goods produced in China. Mr. Romney would end American government procurement—which ensures that nations can compete on an equal basis for government contracts—from Chinese firms until the Chinese government opens up its procurement process to American firms. Furthermore, he would allow Taiwan to buy as many weapons from the United States as it likes. Mr. Obama, on the other hand, has allowed Taiwan to upgrade its existing weapons stock without buying new arms. This is significant because of the complex relationship

---

3. Editorial Board, "A Proper Pivot Towards Asia," *Washington Post*, July 14, 2012, accessed July 31, 2012, http://www.washingtonpost.com/opinions/a-proper-pivot-toward-asia/2012/07/14/gJQA9Y8pkW_story.html.

4. Walter Russell Mead, "Softly, Softly: Beijing Turns Other Cheek—For Now," *American Interest*, November 19, 2011, accessed July 31, 2012, http://blogs.the-american-interest.com/wrm/2011/11/19/softly-softly-beijing-turns-other-cheek-for-now/.

between Taiwan, known as the Republic of China (ROC), and mainland China, known as the People's Republic of China (PRC). After the Chinese civil war, the communist-led PRC took control of mainland China and founded the People's Republic of China in 1949. At that time, the ROC government moved to Taiwan. In 1971, the PRC assumed China's seat at the United Nations, and international recognition of Taiwan has gradually decreased to 23 countries.

Mr. Romney does not oppose the geopolitical pivot strategy, but argues that it should be strengthened and that if elected he would increase the amount of money the United States devotes to ships and the military.[5] Whether Mr. Romney is elected or Mr. Obama is reelected, foreign policy toward China is likely to remain the same. Mr. Romney talks tough about China now, but it is likely he will backtrack from his campaign promises on China much as Mr. Obama did after 2008.

Discussion Questions

1. Why does the author of the article believe that the candidates' comments regarding China are only campaign rhetoric?
2. Why is China a "convenient boogeyman" for presidential candidates?
3. Describe President Obama's "pivot" strategy of containment of China's influence in Asia.

---

5. Mitt Romney, "How I'll Respond to China's Rising Power," *Wall Street Journal*, February 16, 2012, accessed July 31, 2012, http://online.wsj.com/article/SB10001424052970204880404577225340763595570.html?mod=googlenews_wsj.

4. In your opinion, how well do you think President Obama has handled relations with China and Taiwan during his presidency?
5. Do you think that China's influence in the world will increase or remain the same in the twenty-first century?

Executive Power in Foreign Policy

Chad Gholizadeh

Executive power refers to the executive branch's ability to make decisions without the permission or direction of the legislative branch (Congress) and the judicial branch (the Supreme Court). Although Congress and the Supreme Court can limit executive branch actions, often in matters of national security, the president, as the leader of the executive branch, will make an irreversible decision on his own. This might be the decision to assassinate an enemy combatant, or to hold a prisoner without a trial. Throughout the twentieth century, the use of executive power has expanded, and it has also become increasingly controversial, particularly after policies put forth by the administration of President George W. Bush allowed the military to torture several accused terrorists in an effort to extract information from them related to national security. The debate over executive power is a test of the system of checks and balances built into the U.S. Constitution, and it requires the candidates and the American voters to strike a balance between national security and individual liberty.

Since President Barack Obama took office in January 2009, the use of executive power has been particularly controversial in the continued operation of the Guantánamo Bay detention center and the use of unmanned drones for targeted killings.

The Guantánamo Bay detention camp is an interrogation facility located in Guantánamo Bay, Cuba, at a U.S. naval base. Because it is not on American soil, the U.S. government has used Guantánamo as a location for interrogating enemy suspects without giving them trials. At the height of the War on Terror, President Bush used Guantánamo as a place to interrogate suspected terrorists, causing much controversy, especially when the Supreme Court ruled in a series of cases that the detainees were entitled to the basic protections of the Constitution.

During his 2008 presidential campaign, then-senator Obama promised to close the detention center. Once in office, President Obama issued executive orders authorizing the closure of Guantánamo and the transfer of inmates detained there to U.S. prisons.[1] Congress opposed the policies of these executive orders, and has repeatedly added clauses to defense bills prohibiting the transfer of detainees, effectively blocking the shuttering of the facility.[2]

---

1. Barack Obama, "Presidential Memorandum—Closure of Detention Facilities at the Guantanamo Bay Naval Base," The White House, December 15, 2009, accessed July 24, 2012, http://www.whitehouse.gov/the-press-office/presidential-memorandum-closure-dentention-facilities-guantanamo-bay-naval-base.

2. Charles C. Krulak and Joseph P. Hoar, "Guantánamo Forever?" New York Times, December 12, 2011, accessed July 24, 2012, http://www.nytimes.com/2011/12/13/opinion/guantanamo-forever.html.

Governor Mitt Romney has voiced support for the continued use of the Guantánamo Bay detention center, stating that he believes it will prevent detainees from having access to increased procedural tools, such as lawyers.[3]

Another area where the assertion of executive powers is controversial is the use of targeted killings as a counter-terrorism strategy. The first known use of Unmanned Aerial Vehicles (drones) to kill suspected terrorists and insurgents was in 2004 during the Bush administration, but the use of drones has increased steeply under President Obama. Since Mr. Obama took office, the United States has mounted over three hundred drone strikes in Pakistan, Somalia, Yemen, and, allegedly, the Philippines. Drones have been used by the Obama administration in the targeted killings of fighters associated with Al Qaeda, the Taliban, and other militant Islamist groups. The administration also authorized strikes targeting Anwar al-Awlaki and Samir Khan, two American citizens. The use of drones has been controversial because of the legal justification for them presented by the Obama administration, the risk posed to civilians, and the constitutional questions raised by the targeted killing of American citizens, among other reasons.

President Obama has justified the use of drones to perform targeted killings using the original Authorization for Use of Military Force (AUMF) passed by Congress in 2001 after the 9/11 attacks. The administration claims that the AUMF's authorization of "all necessary and appropriate force" against Al Qaeda and associated forces provides enough

---

3. "Romney: 'We Ought to Double Guantánamo," Think Progress, May 16, 2007, accessed July 24, 2012, http://thinkprogress.org/politics/2007/05/16/12919/romney-guantanamo/.

congressional support for the continued use of military force outside of the Afghan arena, where U.S. forces were fighting the terrorist group in the wake of September 11.[4] In addition to the legal justification, there is evidence that the use of drones to kill targets is less dangerous to civilians than other means.[5] The president has claimed that the AUMF's authorization to target worldwide terrorist operatives allows him to form and maintain a list of individuals, including possible American citizens, who can be targeted for these attacks. Attorney General Eric Holder justified this targeting by noting that the constitutional guarantee of "due process" does not require a judicial procedure. Creating a broad framework, Mr. Holder claims that the executive may target an American citizen if, after balancing potential casualties against the government's interests in national security, the person is determined to be a combatant (or a civilian participating in hostilities) of "definite military value," if the anticipated collateral damage is not excessive, and if the targeted killing will not cause unnecessary suffering.[6]

Governor Romney has not criticized the president's framework for drone strikes or disputed any of the powers that he claims. Republican politicians like former Minnesota governor Tim Pawlenty have claimed that Mr. Romney would

4. Jonathan Masters, "Targeted Killing," Council on Foreign Relations, April 30, 2012, accessed July 24, 2012, http://www.cfr.org/counterterrorism/targeted-killings/p9627.

5. Scott Shane, "The Moral Case for Drones," *New York Times*, July 14, 2012, accessed July 24, 2012, http://www.nytimes.com/2012/07/15/sunday-review/the-moral-case-for-drones.html?_r=1&hp.

6. "Text of the Attorney General's National Security Speech," Lawfare, March 5, 2012, accessed July 24, 2012, http://www.lawfareblog.com/2012/03/text-of-the-attorney-generals-national-security-speech/.

"go farther" than Obama on the use of drones,[7] but Mr. Romney himself has not openly claimed that he would expand the size and scope of the drone campaign. He has criticized the president by claiming that Mr. Obama has not been aggressive enough,[8] and it is not clear to what extent he would utilize the legal and material framework set up by President Obama to execute drone strikes to pursue other military goals.

Both candidates, and their parties, seem intent on at least maintaining the current situation with regard to the use of drones. The broad consensus between the parties on this issue means if Mr. Romney wins the 2012 election he will inherit a legal and military framework that interprets the original AUMF as a broad congressional mandate authorizing the president to conduct these strikes. Now that the Obama administration's counterterrorism advisor John Brennan has publicly acknowledged the use of these drones, there may be room for more debate between the candidates about the merits of the attacks. But until that debate happens, the candidates have something they can agree on.

Discussion Questions

1. Define "executive power" in the context of the U.S. political system.

---

7. "Pawlenty: On Foreign Policy Romney Would Be Stronger Than Obama," The Situation Room, CNN, June 6, 2012, accessed July 24, 2012, http://situationroom.blogs.cnn.com/2012/06/06/pawlenty-on-foreign-policy-romney-would-be-stronger-than-obama/.

8. "Middle East," Mitt Romney for President, accessed July 24, 2012, http://www.mittromney.com/issues/middle-east.

2. Describe how Congress has limited President Obama's ability to use executive power to close the Guantánamo Bay facility.
3. Predict the likely course of action regarding Guantánamo Bay if Governor Romney is elected president. Present evidence for your prediction.
4. What are the advantages and disadvantages of using drones in military operations?

Foreign Aid and Development

Ella Saunders-Crivello

With the largest economy in the world, the United States has a unique opportunity to help developing countries through foreign aid. America has a long history of using its wealth to help countries in need. Successful development, however, is not easy, and often in the presidential debates, the intricacies of global interdependence — through multinational corporations, national defense, aid, or loans — get simplified. Globalization does not allow for the possibility of separating global markets from politics.

In a 2010 poll, Americans were asked to estimate how much of the federal budget goes to foreign aid.[1] While the median estimate was 25 percent, the median response for what they thought the "appropriate" percentage should be was only 10 percent. In reality, about 1 percent of the national budget is allotted to foreign aid. Steven Kull, director of the Program on International Policy Attitudes, said about

1. "American Public Vastly Overestimates Amount of U.S. Foreign Aid," World Public Opinion.Org, November 29, 2010, accessed July 24, 2012, http://www.worldpublicopinion.org/pipa/articles/brunitedstatescanadara/670.php?nid=&id=&pnt=670&lb.

the overestimate that it "may be due to Americans hearing more about [recent] aid efforts occurring in Iraq, Afghanistan and Haiti." The actual investment in foreign aid is a small fraction of the discretionary budget. David Kilcullen explains in his book *The Accidental Gorilla* that in personnel terms, the Department of Defense is about 210 times larger than the U.S. Agency of International Development (USAID) and the State Department combined, and it has 350 times as large a budget.[2]

Governor Mitt Romney believes that Americans will be better off cutting foreign aid expenses. In an October 2011 Republican primary debate, Mr. Romney passionately defended the GOP stance of questioning humanitarian assistance. He said, "I happen to think it doesn't make a lot of sense for us to borrow money from the Chinese to go give to another country for humanitarian aid. . . . We ought to get the Chinese to take care of the people that are taking that borrowed money."[3] Mr. Romney's campaign often compares President Barack Obama's policies to those of Europe. He criticizes the Obama administration's foreign assistance efforts as largely squandered by a fragmented Washington bureaucracy.

Mr. Romney does not prioritize encouraging good governance and stability abroad through foreign aid. "Mitt's Plan" regarding Africa, for instance, declares in a nuanced fashion, "a Romney administration will encourage and assist African nations to adopt policies that create business-friendly

---

2. Sarah C. Sullivan, "Poll: Americans Have Inflated View of Foreign Aid," The Rundown, PBS, December 6, 2010, accessed July 24, 2012, http://www.pbs.org/newshour/rundown/2010/12/foreign-aid.html.

3. "Full Transcript CNN Western Republican Presidential Debate," October 18, 2011, accessed July 24, 2012, http://archives.cnn.com/TRANSCRIPTS/1110/18/se.05.html.

environments and combat governmental corruption." His campaign further argues, "greater market access across the continent for U.S. businesses will bolster job creation in Africa as well as in the United States."[4] While the Romney campaign rejects the notion that the United States has an obligation to rely on foreign aid in its international development efforts, Mr. Obama seeks to justify his aid policy by invoking the morality of humanitarianism.

The Obama administration has opposed cutting aid, and the 2011 budget reflects that by putting the United States on a path to double foreign assistance by 2015. The Obama campaign argues for pragmatic budgetary approaches to foreign aid. In Mr. Obama's 2012 campaign, promoting good governance through foreign aid makes sense for a range of foreign policy and development objectives. The Obama administration wants to increase foreign assistance to make investments to combat terrorism, corruption and transnational crime, improve global education and health, reduce poverty, build global food security, expand the Peace Corps, address climate change, stabilize post-conflict states, and reinforce conflict prevention. In a speech promoting good governance in Ghana, President Obama stated, "the true sign of success is not whether we are a source of aid that helps people scrape by—it is whether we are partners in building the capacity for transformational change."[5] The goal remains to expand diplomatic and development capacity while renewing the United States as a global leader.

---

4. "Africa," Mitt Romney for President, accessed July 24, 2012, http://www.mittromney.com/issues/africa.

5. William Wallis, "Obama Calls for Good Governance in Africa," *Financial Times*, July 11, 2009, accessed July 24, 2012, http://www.ft.com/cms/s/0/ce60f8ca-6e0a-11de-8cd0-00144feabdc0.html#axzz1zBFrWLOe.

The Obama administration, however, faced a roadblock in its approach to foreign aid in the Middle East as the Arab Spring unfolded in 2011. Mr. Obama announced that the U.S. government would provide more immediate benefits to support a successful and prospering democracy for the Egyptian people, but this was not well received by the supposed beneficiaries themselves.[6] According to a February 2012 Gallup poll, seven in ten Egyptians say they oppose U.S. economic aid to Egypt while three-quarters oppose the State Department's efforts to fund Egypt's pro-democracy groups.[7] This may have been because Egyptians perceived that the Obama administration was aiming to use aid as a tool to advance U.S. strategic interests.

The Council on Foreign Relations' Isobel Coleman suggests that, led by USAID, there will be some major trends likely to endure no matter who is elected president in November.[8] These trends include a move away from the last decade's emphasis on Iraq and Afghanistan as well as more emphasis on collaboration with the private sector. In a June 2012 op-ed, President Bill Clinton argued that the debate on foreign aid

---

6. Warren Strobel, "Obama Set to Speed Aid to Egypt: Official," Reuters, January 25, 2012, accessed July 24, 2012, http://www.reuters.com/article/2012/01/25/us-davos-usa-egypt-idUSTRE80024G20120125.

7. Ahmed Younis and Mohamed Younis, "Most Egyptians Oppose U.S. Economic Aid: Most Favor Aid from Arab Nations," Gallup World, February 6, 2012, accessed July 24, 2012, http://www.gallup.com/poll/152471/Egyptians-Oppose-Economic-Aid.aspx?utm_source=alert&utm_medium=email&utm_campaign=syndication&utm_content=morelink&utm_term=Politics%20-%20World.

8. Isobel Coleman, "Foreign Aid II: USAID, Development Trends, and the Presidential Campaign," Democracy in Development Blog, Council on Foreign Relations, April 6, 2012, accessed July 24, 2012, http://blogs.cfr.org/coleman/2012/04/06/foreign-aid-ii-usaid-development-trends-and-the-presidential-campaign/.

should include a reevaluation of the end goals. He said, "When governments, businesses, and non-governmental organizations [NGOs] work together to share expertise and forge creative solutions, everyone can win, not only the people in developing nations but also the corporations and philanthropists involved, by diversifying their businesses, growing their markets, training more potential workers, and, for NGOs, expanding their impact."[9] The historical trends in foreign aid, along with the irrepressible force of globalization, are perhaps greater factors than the positions of the candidates. More significant in the 2012 presidential election is the question of how Americans see themselves as global citizens.

Discussion Questions

1. In your opinion, should the delivery of foreign aid to developing countries be a priority for the next president of the United States?
2. Describe how Governor Romney's position on foreign aid and development differs from President Obama's.
3. Do you agree with Governor Romney that Americans will be "better off" if foreign aid is cut?
4. Why do you think Americans wrongly perceive the foreign aid budget to be 25 times larger than it actually is?
5. Does the United States have a moral responsibility to give aid to poorer countries?

---

9. Bill Clinton, "Africa—A Continent Ready to Fulfil Its Potential," *London Evening Standard*, June 27, 2012, accessed July 24, 2012, http://www. standard.co.uk/comment/bill-clinton-africa--a-continent-ready-to-fulfil-its-potential-7892725.html.

Iran

Diana Li

In the 1950s, Iran began developing a nuclear power program, originally with the support of the United States. Today however, 23 years after the fall of the Shah of Iran and the rise of the Islamic Republic, the United Nations and many governments, including the United States, have expressed concern that Iranian leaders may actually be developing a nuclear bomb. The Iranian government claims that its nuclear program is simply for civilian energy purposes, has ratified the Nuclear Nonproliferation Treaty, and has technically submitted to International Atomic Energy Agency inspections (conducted by an external body). Still, widespread concern that Iran will eventually create a bomb has turned U.S. foreign policy toward Iran into a key issue that the presidential candidates must address in their campaigns.

One of the issues to consider is the United States' relationship with Israel. Iranian officials have publicly declared that they do not believe Israel has a right to exist. Anything short of what Israel sees as the full cooperation of the United States to rebuff Iran's attempts to obtain a nuclear weapon potentially undermines a historically strong U.S.-Israel relationship. Governor Mitt Romney has repeatedly accused President Barack Obama of being soft on Iran, but Mr.

Obama declared at the annual American Israel Public Affairs Committee in March 2012 that he "will not hesitate to use force when it is necessary to defend the United States and its interests," ensuring those at the conference that a military strike will always be an option.[1]

A nuclear Iran might also negatively influence the prospects for peace in the Middle East. It would likely spark and accelerate a regional arms race, if not a regional race to obtain the bomb itself. This stirring of Middle East tensions would likely undermine a large part of the United States' previous work in stabilizing the region. If Mr. Obama wants to continue to claim progress in the Middle East, he must consider what a nuclear Iran would imply with regard to regional stability. Mr. Romney has capitalized on this fear among Americans of a nuclear Iran, arguing that disaster could strike beyond just the Middle East and that Iranian use of the bomb would globalize the conflict. Furthermore, Mr. Romney can point to the continuing instability in the Middle East as a failure of Obama's foreign policy.

A final issue for consideration is how the future president can effectively combat Iran with (or without) international cooperation. Currently, the United States is acting largely in cooperation with a number of other countries by imposing round after round of economic sanctions—trade penalties meant to influence the target country's policies—against Iran. However, these sanctions are only effective if Iran truly cannot find other trading partners. If nations with large economies do not participate in the sanctions, Iran

---

1. Christi Parsons, "Obama: U.S. 'Will Not Hesitate to Use Force' Against Iran," *New York Times*, March 4, 2012, accessed July 23, 2012, http://articles.latimes.com/2012/mar/04/news/la-pn-obama-aipac-20120304.

can simply circumvent sanctions by finding a willing trade partner. Mitt Romney has made it very clear that he is willing to act independently of other countries, and when asked how he would check Iran's nuclear program, he responded, "Until Iran ceases its nuclear bomb program, I will press for ever-tightening sanctions, acting with other countries if we can, but alone if we must . . . I will buttress my diplomacy with a military option."[2] President Obama, however, has made it a key point of his agenda to keep engagement open as an option and at least attempt to incorporate other countries in his policies.

Moving forward, the future president will have to adopt a firm stance regarding Iran. The current policy is comprised of a number of different sanctions imposed on the country, with the United Nations, the European Union, and individual nations acting both independently and together against Iran. Although it is difficult to say how effective sanctions have been, they have made it comparatively more difficult for the Iranian government to obtain materials necessary for a weapons program. Though Iranian leaders' current intentions remain unclear, the hope is that in the long run, the sanctions will be harmful enough to discourage and deter them from further pursuing their nuclear weapons program. Many supporters of Israel publicly advocate for a military option, pointing to the continuing Iranian nuclear ambitions as evidence that sanctions have failed. Both presidential candidates will have to consider how seriously they take the

---

2. Mitt Romney, "How I Would Check Iran's Nuclear Ambition," *Washington Post*, March 5, 2012, accessed July 23, 2012, http://www.washingtonpost.com/opinions/mitt-romney-how-i-would-check-irans-nuclear-ambition/2012/03/05/gIQAneYItR_story.html.

possibility of a military strike beyond simply saying that it is an option that they are willing to pursue given the appropriate circumstances.

Despite the differences between President Obama and Governor Romney, their public stances regarding Iran may not actually be as divergent as some people portray them to be: both of them have said that they are willing to consider a military option, that they support strengthened sanctions, and that they must prevent Iran from obtaining a nuclear weapon. Mr. Obama began his presidency by pledging a policy of "engagement" that included a "new emphasis on respect,"[3] but he has clearly started to discuss other possibilities beyond just negotiating with Iran. Mr. Obama does not want to risk a nuclear Iran, which will make him look soft on terrorism, whereas Mr. Romney must caution against looking like an American war hawk who will exacerbate tensions.

Discussion Questions

1. To what extent does the Iranian nuclear program affect the United States' relations with Israel?
2. Do you believe that President Obama is willing to use military force against Iran to protect Israel? Give evidence to justify your opinion.
3. Identify the risks and merits of Governor Romney's unilateral approach regarding Iran.

---

3. Brian Knowlton, "In Interview, Obama Talks of 'New Approach' to Iran," *New York Times*, January 11, 2009, accessed July 23, 2012, http://www. nytimes.com/2009/01/12/us/politics/12iran.html.

4. Overall, what are the similarities in the positions of both President Obama and Governor Romney when it comes to Iran?
5. If he were elected president, how might Governor Romney's "zero-sum game" approach to foreign policy worsen relations with Iran?

Russia

Saskia Brechenmacher

Relations between the United States and Russia since the collapse of the Soviet Union have been marked by periods of increased cooperation and engagement as well as considerable diplomatic hurdles and disagreements. The two countries are no longer the strong antagonists that they used to be and now share numerous common interests, such as the struggle against Islamic fundamentalism, terrorism, and nuclear proliferation, and the challenge of economic competitiveness in a globalized world economy. Nevertheless, relations between the two countries reached a new low point during the second administration of President George W. Bush, when disagreements over the future of strategic arms limitations, missile defense in Europe, enlargement of the North Atlantic Treaty Organization to the east, and the Georgian-Russian conflict dominated the agenda.

Four years later, relations have improved, even though the Russian government remains suspicious of American motives and continues to obstruct U.S. efforts in the Middle East through its veto power in the UN Security Council. However, the fundamental question for the United States with regard to Russia remains how to balance cooperation in order to advance U.S. interests on issues like Afghanistan and Iran with concerns over Russia's human rights abuses and undemocratic system of government.

President Barack Obama's original foreign policy objective was to "reset" the relationship with Russia after a period of increasingly strained relations between the White House and the Kremlin, an effort that was welcomed by Dmitry Medvedev, predecessor to current Russian president Vladimir Putin. The Obama administration's policy toward Russia has been marked by caution, pragmatism, and a strong willingness to engage rather than confront. Core achievements of Mr. Obama's "reset" policy have been the signing of a new strategic arms control treaty (START), the finalization of a civilian nuclear cooperation pact, an agreement on tougher sanctions against Iran, and the expanded American supply route to Afghanistan through former Soviet territory. In 2011, Mr. Obama chose Michael McFaul, the architect of the "reset policy," as the new U.S. ambassador to Moscow. Ambassador McFaul is an adviser from the President's inner circle, rather than a career diplomat, and so his appointment signaled Mr. Obama's desire to keep Russian-American relations a foreign policy priority.[1]

Lately the relationship has suffered from Russia's continued military support of the authoritarian regime in Syria. Since early in 2011, the Syrian government has been violently suppressing a popular uprising, creating what has been described by many as a civil war. Although the U.S. military is not directly involved in the conflict, President Obama has publicly condemned the Syrian government, and it has been reported that the Central Intelligence Agency is helping to

---

1. Peter Baker, "Policy Adviser Tapped to Become U.S. Ambassador in Russia," *New York Times*, May 29, 2012, accessed July 27, 2012, http://www.nytimes.com/2011/05/29/world/europe/29envoy.html.

drive arms to the Syrian opposition.[2] Russia, however, has strongly supported the Syrian government by vetoing proposed United Nations sanctions and sending direct arms shipments to the Syrian regime. In the short term, at least, this has put significant strain on Russian-American relations.

President Obama's policy of engagement has also been criticized for its uncertainty with regard to a reconfigured U.S. missile defense system in Europe and the diminished pressure it is exerting on the Kremlin to enforce democratic reforms and stop intimidating former Soviet states such as Georgia and Ukraine. Human rights advocates accuse the president of ignoring the erosion of Russian democracy, as he refrained from commenting on the corrupt Russian parliamentary elections and subsequent protest movement, and instead congratulated Mr. Putin on his reelection in March 2012 without further criticism of Russia's human rights record.

Although the reelection of Mr. Putin may put new strains on the relationship between the Kremlin and the White House, Mr. Obama's Russia policy is likely to be marked by significant continuity if he is reelected in November. This policy is based on the recognition that the two countries share common interests, that engagement with Moscow can produce win-win outcomes, and that the United States can seek cooperation with the Russian government while simultaneously strengthening ties with Russian civil society.[3] Mr. Obama's first term in

---

2. Eric Schmitt, "C.I.A. Said to Aid in Steering Arms to Syrian Opposition," *New York Times*, June 21, 2012, accessed July 25, 2012, http://www.nytimes. com/2012/06/21/world/middleeast/cia-said-to-aid-in-steering-arms-to-syrian-rebels.html.

3. U.S. Department of State, "State's Gordon at Senate Hearing on U.S. Policy in Russia," December 14, 2011, accessed July 27, 2012, http://www.uspolicy. be/headline/state%E2%80%99s-gordon-senate-hearing-us-policy-russia.

office has proven that his administration views Putin as a "transactional" leader who will cooperate if he perceives such cooperation to be in Russia's interest and whose involvement is crucial in addressing the current crises in Iran, Afghanistan, and Syria. The president's policy priorities for 2012 also include the strengthening of economic ties with Russia. His administration supports the Russian accession to the World Trade Organization and currently aims at pushing Congress to repeal the Jackson–Vanik amendment, which has blocked Russia from receiving Permanent Normal Trade Status with the United States since 1974.

Governor Mitt Romney's campaign has been highly critical of Mr. Obama's foreign policy and national security record, yet U.S. policy toward Russia represents one of the few foreign policy areas in which Mr. Romney's approach differs from that of the Obama administration. In a CNN interview in March 2012, Mr. Romney controversially declared that he considered Russia to be the United States' "number one geopolitical foe," thereby indicating his conviction that, even in the post-Soviet era, Russia's actions in the international sphere remain fundamentally opposed to U.S. interests. This statement did not go unnoticed in Moscow, and Mr. Romney was criticized by leading Republican and Democratic foreign policy experts for failing to recognize the changed nature of Russian-American relations. Mr. Romney, however, partially shares President George W. Bush's view of foreign policy as a zero sum game.[4] His foreign policy stance on Russian-American relations conveys his larger belief that national security threats are

---

4. "Mitt Romney's Russia," *Harvard Crimson*, May 23, 2012, accessed July 27, 2012, http://www.thecrimson.com/article/2012/5/23/romney-russia-perspective/.

closely tied to economic power, which in Russia's case stems from the country's vast oil and gas reserves. According to Mr. Romney's official campaign statements, he views Russia as a "destabilizing force on the world stage" that needs to be tempered.[5]

He has therefore characterized President Obama's attempt to "reset" Russian-American relations as a foreign policy failure that has led to excessive American concessions without Russian reciprocation. He has criticized in particular Mr. Obama's withdrawal from the missile-defense system in Central and Eastern Europe and the signing of the New START treaty on nuclear disarmament in 2010 as steps that have weakened America's position without eliciting further cooperation from Moscow.[6] On the contrary, Mr. Romney views Moscow's continued opposition to U.S. efforts in the Middle East and Syria in particular as a sign that the Russian government is not a useful ally on the world stage.

Governor Romney's current policy proposals on Russia are a mix of realist and neoconservative approaches. On the one hand, he aims to build stronger military, diplomatic, and economic relationships with Central Asia in order to move these states beyond Russia's sphere of influence. On the other hand, he names democracy promotion and the strengthening of civil society within Russia as one of his top priorities, and he has repeatedly criticized Mr. Obama for making concessions to Mr. Putin's authoritarian regime. If elected, Governor Romney would review the implementation of the New START treaty, which in his view puts a disproportionate burden on the United

---

5. "Russia," Mitt Romney for President, accessed July 27, 2012, http://www.mittromney.com/issues/russia.

6. Ibid.

States, and would work toward reducing European energy dependence on Russia.

Discussion Questions

1. According to the author of the article, what are the four "common interests" that the United States and Russia share?
2. Has President Obama been successful in improving relations with Russia and promoting U.S. interests there?
3. To what extent has the Syrian conflict affected Russian-American relations?
4. Do you agree with Governor Romney's position that Russia's vast oil and gas resources threaten U.S. interests? Explain your position.

Contributors

Saskia Brechenmacher studied political science and Slavic studies at Brown University and is a junior fellow at the Carnegie Endowment for International Peace in Washington, D.C.

A.J. Carver earned an MA in empirical and theoretical economics from Université Paris 1 Panthéon-Sorbonne.

Dean DeChiaro has a BA from Occidental College, where he majored in History and minored in Classical Studies.

Ross Duncan studied economics at McGill University and is an analyst at Alberta Health Services.

Chad Gholizadeh is a second-year law student at Brooklyn Law School.

Andrew Howard is an assistant professor at Central State University.

Robert Hunter graduated from Brown University with a BA in American studies and education, and has worked at the Vera Institute's Center on Youth Justice.

David Katz received his MPA in environmental science and policy from Columbia University's School of International and Public Affairs, and works for SunRay Power LLC.

Diana Li is a student at Yale University majoring in history and economics.

Ted Mateoc is a student at McGill University majoring in political science and history.

Shawn Patterson is a PhD candidate in political science at the University of California, Los Angeles.

Nathan Rifkin is a student at Middlebury College.

Ella Saunders-Crivello graduated from New York University's Gallatin School with a BA in Social Enterprise and International Relations.

Christine Seo has a JD/MBA from Fordham University.

Roger Sollenberger is an instructor at Georgia College.

Denise Yu recently graduated from Columbia with a BA in political science.

Bruce Lee Zellers is currently an American history teacher at the Greenhills School in Ann Arbor, Michigan and a special lecturer at Oakland University. He earned a BA from Oakland University and an MA in history from Clark University. He has reviewed books for several publications, most recently *Michigan War Studies Review*.